VICTOI

ROOSEVELT SARGENT

This book is dedicated to Desiree, Eurico, Arkita, and Janell. Something in my soul shifted every time I first laid eyes on each of you. We share so much more than blood, genes, and character traits. You are my heart. You have given me all the inspiration that I will ever need to never give up in life. I want you to know that nothing is impossible. Imagine big and pursue your wildest dreams. Keep your faith in God and never give up on Him and I promise He will never let you down. This victory is for you.

~Pops

Author Info:

Facebook – Roosevelt Sargent

Like Page – Victorious Underdog

Twitter - @rosargent73

Email – rosargent@victoriousunderdog.org

www.victoriousunderdog.org

## Prologue

*June 15*

Seattle, Washington

I eased the sky blue Camaro through the streets of the inner city with no place to be and plenty of time to get there. Windows down and speakers thumping as we shouted the words to our favorite NWA song, "Fuck tha police! Fuck, fuck, fuck tha police!" My homies and I passed around a bottle of Wild Irish Rose, the sweet wine going down like Kool-Aid. We were just sixteen and out on a Saturday night; cruising the town looking for a good time. What in the world could possibly happen to four boys who weren't looking for any trouble?

The Camaro belonged to Marvin, a homeboy from high school. He was a straight up gangsta with a crazy attitude, but he was cool with me and I was renting an apartment with him until I got things sorted out. A few hours earlier, Marvin had tossed me the keys and said, "Hey Rose, I got a broad coming over and I need you to get ghost for a while. Take my car and cruise around, but don't be back before midnight, ya hear?"

I caught the keys with both hands. "Thanks, bro, and don't worry. I'll stay gone all night with a ride like this." In no time at all I'd grabbed my stuff and headed for the door. But just as my hand undid the two deadbolts, something strong gripped my shoulder. "Rose," a dark voice whispered in my ear, "Don't fuck up my ride, got it?"

Without turning my head, I said, "No problem Marv. 'Don't fuck up' is my middle name."
"Yeah, that's what I like to hear. I'd hate to plant roses over my favorite Rose."
I grinned nervously, but said nothing. After all, I was just a lowlife street hustler; Marvin was a mad dog ...a killer. Where I might get mad and call someone a 'mutha fucka', he'd just off 'em with a .38. It was his default response. "Yo, Marv, you gon pay me that twenty bucks?" *Blam!* "Marvin, you ain't messin' wif my girl, are ya?" *Blam!* "Hey asshole, your car door dinged my car." *Blam!* That's why when I say I eased the car through the streets, I was driving as carefully as possible—or at least as carefully as a sixteen year old with plenty of Wild Irish Rose coursing through his veins could.

In the car were my three homies: Tommy, Kenny, and Pig. I'd scooped them up nearly as soon as I'd stuck the key in the ignition. Pig had brought along the bottle of Wild Irish Rose, which we promptly used to christen my Camaro—*Marvin's Camaro*.

We'd gotten to the point where we were just cruising around, killing time, when suddenly, a black Buick Regal pulled up next to us and rolled down their windows. Two Mexican cholos in the front seat were throwing signs at us.

"Hey, what the fuck! Rose, are you seeing this?!"

Kenny was next to me in the front seat staring at the esses, who were just inches from our passenger side.

"Yeah, I see it! Hit 'em back up."

Kenny began yelling at them and they yelled back, daring us to pull over so they could whip our asses. I sped up, got in front of the Buick, and swerved over to a side street where I slammed on the brakes. Seconds later the Buick skidded to a stop behind us, and the two cholos jumped out, heading for our car.

"C'mon, ya'll, let's get wit these fools!" I yelled.

Kenny and I opened the two doors and sprung to our feet. Right behind us were Pig and Tommy who had to climb over the folded seats to get out. As the Mexican coming at me started swinging wildly for my jaw, I landed a blow to the side of his head. When he saw Pig behind me, I could tell he knew he'd miscalculated the amount of people in the two-door Camaro. In less than a minute, he was lying flat on his back, bleeding everywhere, and moaning. I looked over at Kenny and Tommy—they'd just finished off their opponent, who was now in the same state as our attacker.

"That was easy work," Kenny said.

"Yeah, look at 'em now, trying to bang on somebody...dumb asses," said Pig.

Tommy laughed. "Well I don't know about you, but to the victor go the spoilers. Let's check out their car."

I shook my head still breathing hard. "It ain't *spoilers*, bro, but go ahead. They got it coming."

Kenny and Tommy climbed into the Buick and began rifling through everything, filling a paper bag from a nearby fast food joint with all the booty they could carry. Pig patted me on the shoulder. "Rose, nice shot you got in before I got to 'im." He held the bottle of Wild Irish Rose, drinking deeply between gulps of fresh air.

"Yeah," I said. "The first shot makes all the difference." I walked back to the Camaro and turned off the headlights. There was no sense in attracting any police.

"Still bro, you got a good punch, remind me not to...

I turned around to say something to Pig, but saw the Mexican just getting to his feet and about to jump Pig from behind.

"Look out. Pig, he's back up!"

On sheer reflex, Pig spun around and crashed the bottle over the Mexican's head, causing him to fall face-first to the asphalt, blood streaming from the sharp pieces of glass sticking out of his face. It looked bad, really bad.

"Hey, ya'll," I yelled. "Get the fuck out of their car, 'cuz I'm getting outta here. Now!"

Kenny and Tommy had seen the blow and were already scrambling out of the Mexicans' car and sprinting to the Camaro. When they jumped in, we burned off.

"Shit, Rose, that was close! If you hadn't a warned me, he'd a got me good. Sho nuff."

"Yeah, that was a close one. 'Cept now we got nothing to drink."

Kenny spoke up. "Go to the 7-Eleven I told you 'bout. I'll go in and see if I can get some forties."

By now, the memory of the fight was already fading. I'd been in fights before and they didn't hang with me for long as they used to. Ten minutes later, I was relaxed and driving the speed limit to avoid getting pulled over. We arrived and Kenny told me to park across the street, not right up on the store. Apparently, they sold to underage neighborhood kids, but not to folks in cars in case they were cops.

Kenny pointed at me. "Rose, come in with me. You two stay in the car."

I turned around to both Pig and Tommy. "Yeah, and don't put a scratch on this car while I'm gone or I'll kill you before Marvin kills me."

"Yeah, whatever," Pig smirked.

We closed the doors and casually walked across the street. "Just let me find the right guy. And let me do the talking. Besides, I got the Mexicans' money and the beer's on them tonight."

"Okay," I said. "Sounds like a plan to me."

Kenny and I went inside the store and I hung right behind him as he scoped out the employees. Luckily, the store was full of people, so we didn't look like we were casing the joint. This went on for a long few minutes, as all I could do was stare at the customers holding the very same beer we wanted to buy. Then, for some strange reason, I glanced out the window and saw it.

"Ken, *look!*"

Kenny turned towards the window and saw what I was looking at. "What?! Let's go."

We ran out the store just in time to see these huge Samoan gangsters all dressed in red surrounding the Camaro. There must have been at least ten of them. By now, two of them were on the hood jumping up and down crushing the metal into the engine block. Then one of them—who probably weighed three hundred pounds—jumped on the roof and it sunk a foot into the interior cabin.

*Crash!*

My jaw dropped as another one swung a bat into the passenger window shattering it into a million pieces. Another one held a tire iron and he was alternating between hitting the windows and the metal exterior. Occasionally he connected with some fiberglass and shattered it, too. As we got closer, we could see the terrified faces of Pig and Tommy convinced they were about to be crushed to death.

I ran over to the scene staying a good distance from the boys in red. "Please, please leave my homies alone. Man, *please*, just let 'em get out of the car."

Two Samoans stopped swinging at the car and turned towards me. "What'd you say?"

A spotlight hit all of us. I glanced over and saw the flashing lights of two police cars as they turned onto the street and raced towards us. When I looked back at the Samoans, they'd scattered like cockroaches in a dark room when the lights come on. Two cops jumped out with guns drawn and ordered Kenny and I onto the ground. A minute later Tommy and Pig were out of the car and either in cuffs or zip ties. The police cuffed me too, and I leaned against one of the police cars.

Cops were everywhere trying to sort it out. Eventually, one of them approached and asked me my story. When I told him everything I knew, he unlocked the cuffs. "We talked to witnesses who said it was your car they were destroying."

*Actually it's Marvin's,* I thought to myself, *who's gonna want to carve me into pieces real slow.* But no sense in bringing that up right now, at least not until after I'd cleared the Canadian border.

"Yeah," I said as I rubbed my wrists. "Me and Kenny went into the 7-Eleven to buy some be...uh, buh-beef jerky and next thing I know these Samoans roll up, and start destroying the car for no reason at all. We didn't do nothing, I swear!"

He was taking notes. "Okay, I get you. Have you seen them before?"

"No, never. They're all dressed in red and huge. It was crazy. They got us mistaken for someone else."

"Probably. It may be your sky blue Camaro. There're not a lot of those rolling around in this hood."

"I guess, probably the only one."

The cop nodded. "For sure. Say, where have you boys been all night? What else you been up to?"

I blinked several times. "Uhh nothin', just cruising around...not causing any trouble."

"Hmm, I see. Been drinking any Wild Irish Rose tonight...uh...Mr. Roosevelt *Sargent*?"

My heart stopped—literally.

"Huh?"

"I said, 'been drinking any Wild Irish Rose tonight, *Rose*'?"

I shook my head. "N-no. W-why?"

The cop lowered his notebook and stared directly into my eyes. "Oh just asking. Someone saw a sky blue Camaro leaving a black Buick Regal with two Mexican kids bleeding all over the road. One of them had pieces of glass from a Wild Irish Rose bottle in his face. The coroner's hauling him to the morgue so they can notify his next of kin. You got any next of kin I can notify while your homies over there spill the beans on that dead kid?"

Having long ago stopped breathing, I swallowed hard hoping somehow to generate some saliva. I could see all three of my boys were separated and talking to different police officers. If one of them rolled, we were all dead. But if we all kept our mouths shut, we just might make it. I couldn't decide which way to go. When I saw the evil grin on the cop's face, I made my decision.

"Don't know nothin' about it, sorry. Can I go now?"

He shook his head. "Nah. There's been a murder Mr. *Sargent*. The only place you're going is downtown to talk to Mr. *Lieutenant*." Chuckling, he added, "Pretty sure he outranks you."

Pulse pounding, I hung my head in deep fear. This was the worst trouble I'd ever been in. Now, like my Mom and Dad, I was about to face prison time—a lot of it. Soon I'd be just another nameless black face lost to the system.

## Chapter One

From the beginning of time, folks have argued over and debated the true cause of crime. "Why does a young man pick up a gun and rob someone?" "What makes a person turn to a life of crime?" "Why don't they apply their talents to making an honest living?" I certainly don't have a PhD in criminology, anthropology, or psychology, but I do have a degree in shit, the nasty, deep stuff. That's because I was born into a world of it—a baby with zero chance of climbing out of a massive stinking pile. So as you read my story, even though you may not have a PhD either, see if you can figure out one of the causes of crime. And feel free to compare yourself to me and see if you would've made different decisions.

Starting when I was born doesn't really tell the whole story. To do it right we have to start long before that, all the way back to my maternal grandmother, Georgia Walker. Although Grandma started having babies at fifteen (my mother being the first), our story starts when she was twenty-eight on a weekend when BB King was coming into town. At the time, Grandma and my grandfather had separated, but they were working on getting back together. She was hoping they would soon be living together again, not the least because she needed the income to help raise her six kids and, of course, she loved the man. Well, she knew how much my grandfather loved BB King and bought a couple of tickets as a surprise. They were both disappointed when, at the last minute, his boss called him in to work overtime.

Grandma went to the concert anyway, and as BB was riffing through some string bending blues, she made her way to the bathroom. Along the way, she bumped into a happy couple kissing and snuggling away. Suddenly she did a double take as she realized the man was her husband. She was in total shock and within seconds, she was reaching into her purse and pulling out a pistol. Carefully raising the weapon to his chest, she fired once, shooting him dead on the spot. After he had crumpled to the ground, witnesses said she spit on him and said, "There's your divorce, nigga." Then she turned to the woman, pistol in hand, and said, "You can have him now. He's all yours." There was nothing in the police report to indicate if the woman, who surely knew she was next, pissed her pants. With that, Grandma walked away, completing her trip to the bathroom.

The police immediately arrested my grandmother and tried her in front of a jury. This was a crime of passion and the jury convicted her of manslaughter, but apparently, the laws were very different back then because even though she went to prison, she served less than a year.

Then there's my paternal grandfather Roosevelt Sargent Sr. He was a hard worker and certainly no criminal. Everyone loved him. And by that, I mean *everyone*. They stopped counting at twenty-six, which was the number of children that he's rumored to have fathered with a wide variety of women. I think he must have considered himself a farmer, spreading his seeds everywhere.

My father, named Roosevelt Sargent Jr. (nicknamed June which was short for Junior), had seven children with six different women. He wasn't quite as productive as his father was, but still I guess the adulterer doesn't fall far from the family tree. Out of his seven children, I was number four. I called him Pops, but believe me he was very different from a good guy. Even though he did well in Bible classes and at school during his younger years, he quickly moved into drugs and crime and never looked back. Mom—Arkita Walker—was eighteen when she gave birth to me. I was her first. Pops was twenty-three, but he had better things to do than raise a kid. So, Mom took me home from Dameron Hospital in Stockton, California to a drafty, cheap apartment where it didn't take long for me to catch pneumonia. I went back to the hospital where I clung to life for three weeks, battling a super high temperature and occasional seizures. For some reason—one I wouldn't fully understand until many years later—I survived.

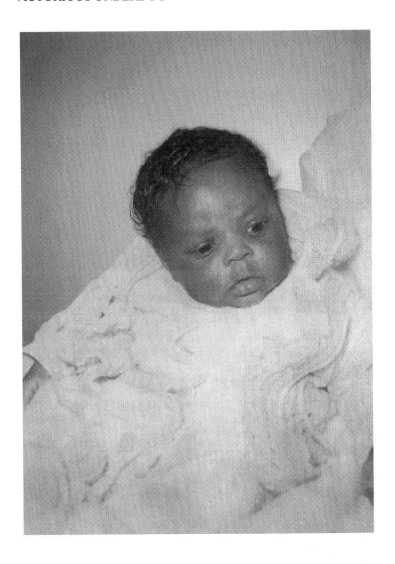

Once I was home, things weren't much better.
Yelling, screaming, and fighting were on the daily
menu. Finally, Mom had had enough. She needed to go
somewhere new and get a fresh start, some place

VICTORIOUS UNDERDOG

where she thought the odds of having a successful life would be just a little bit better. I was only nineteen months old when she chose to move to Seattle, Washington, a place where my Grandma Georgia's brother, Uncle John, lived. He was willing to take us in and help her get that fresh start. We settled into Seattle for about five months when Pops decided to come up and reconcile. Actually, it was just another place for him to commit crimes and do drugs.

Everything seemed to be stabilizing until a particular day, which I'll never forget. I was four years old and riding the preschool bus on the way home from school. It was a typical Seattle day, overcast but not raining. The bus pulled right in front of my house where normally, Mom would be standing on the sidewalk waiting for me to get off. This day was different, though, very different.

As the bus pulled up to the house, I noticed that my mother wasn't standing in her usual place. This was frightening. Then I saw several police cars parked on the street directly in front of our house. The bus driver stopped at the usual spot—just on the other side of the police cars—and let me off. As he pulled away, I walked into the house to see Mom, Pops, and Auntie Sherry (Mom's sister), all standing there in handcuffs, surrounded by police officers. I can't begin to explain the indelible mark this made on the mind of a shocked four year old.

Later, it was explained to me they were being arrested for armed robbery. The first happened late one night when Pops and Auntie Sherry were walking home from the store. They noticed an old lady getting out of her car with some bags in obvious need of help. Pops asked the lady if they could help her carry the bags and she agreed. They grabbed the bags and followed the lady to the front door. When she opened it, Pops pushed her into the house and forced her into a chair where he told the old lady they weren't going to hurt her, but they were going to take a few things. He snatched up a knife from the kitchen and cut the cord from the vacuum cleaner to tie her to the chair. Auntie Sherry had never done anything like this and before she knew what was happening, Pops was already in action, and Auntie Sherry just went with it. They took a couple hundred dollars in cash and rummaged through the house, filling pillowcases with jewelry and other valuables. One was a very nice crystal tabletop ornament, which later became a decorative piece on our table.

The second robbery took place after a female acquaintance informed them of an old lady she knew who kept a lot of cash under her mattress. A few weeks after the first robbery, they did their second. This time Mom was present with Pops and Auntie Sherry. They knocked on the door and the old lady answered. As soon as the door swung open, they rushed in and proceeded to execute the same plan as the first robbery. They tied her to a chair, rummaged through her place and took valuables. When they came to the bed, they were stunned to find no cash under the mattress. By the time they were done, all they'd found was $13.

A week later, someone identified them. When the police came to pick them up for the second robbery, they saw the crystal piece sitting on our table. After a search, they found more of the things from the first robbery, linking them to that one, too. Because Pops used a knife to cut the cord from the vacuum, the police classified it as armed robbery.

Auntie Sherry had a daughter named Salina who we called Kandy; she was one year younger than I was and was staying with us. With all three adults in jail, that left Kandy and me fending for ourselves, which at ages four and three, was impossible. Kandy's father came and picked us up to live with him while we waited to see what the courts would do with our parents. Sure enough, they went to prison—for years. Exactly how many they'd have to serve, we couldn't tell because it depended on their behavior and the kindness of the parole board. But one thing was clear: my parents were long gone with an emphasis on *long*.

Days after they were shipped off to prison, I stood at the bus station waiting on Auntie Pam (another of Mom's sisters) who was coming up from Stockton. She was going to take us back there to live with my Grandma, the pistol-packing momma who was now out of prison. When the Greyhound bus arrived, Auntie Pam got off and said, "Okay, let's get you two on the bus. It's turning around and heading back down south. Is this all you got?"

Kandy and I tightly held small bags full of everything we owned to our chests. We fearfully nodded as a new bus driver walked past us and yelled, "All aboard!"

"Come on," she said yanking us onto the bus by our arms and into a seat. Moments later, the bus eased out of the station and past our neighborhood. I looked out the window as my life and everything I'd known was flying by, disappearing like my parents had. I don't know who was more scared—Kandy or me. Both of us were having our worlds turned upside down.

***

Grandma may have killed someone, and spoke harshly most of the time, but her heart was huge when it came to family. From the moment I arrived, she started encouraging me, filling me with helpful words. It was truly the first time I'd heard anything positive. "Roosevelt, you're special. You're different. You don't know it, but you have something to offer the world." Later, when I trusted everyone a little too much and jumped headfirst into relationships, she taught me the difference between a true friend and an associate. She taught me how to be careful when I used the term 'friend.' And she really believed in me.

At some point she began calling me 'Man.' She said I was uniquely sharp and advanced for my age, carrying myself like a man. To prove her point, earlier in life when I was five, she gave me a note with the exact change and sent me to the store to pick up a pack of cigarettes. Of course, it was a tight community and they knew my grandmother and the fact that I lived with her. When I brought back her cigarettes, she marveled at the accomplishment, congratulating me, although honestly, it would've been hard to mess up.

One day I was playing with the upstairs neighbor, when we decided to walk a block to the corner store to get a Jolly Rancher candy stick. I asked Grandma for permission and she handed me a dime telling me to go have fun. To my disappointment, they were all out of Jolly Ranchers. I looked across the street and wondered if the other store might have some. While my friend was busy selecting his candy, I headed out the door to cross the street, looking both ways before I stepped off the sidewalk. Even so, there was a car parked on my left, which prevented me from seeing if any cars were coming. I did my best to look around it and saw everything was clear, so I took off running as fast as I could toward the other side. However, I apparently hadn't seen everything. Here I was in the middle of the street and sure enough, there was a car coming straight at me. The collision sent my small body flying through the air, twisting my head so it hit the pavement first. I was knocked unconscious.

When I woke up, I was on a stretcher surrounded by a crowd of people. I looked over and saw Grandma standing there in her robe, crying uncontrollably as they loaded me into the ambulance. I still wasn't sure what was going on. When I got to the hospital, they told me a car had hit me. After the doctors looked at the X-rays, they were convinced they must have made a mistake: the X-rays showed no broken bones. They ordered another round. After a second set produced the same results, they looked at each other, shrugged their shoulders, and said, "Son, it's a miracle. You have no broken bones." They treated a few scrapes and kept me in the hospital for two days while they called an X-ray technician to check out the machine. Eventually, they let me go home.

The next time I wanted to go to the store, Grandma came with me. Suddenly, a man came up to her and said, "Excuse me, are you related to this kid, the one who got hit by the car the other day?"

She nodded. "Yes, he's my grandson. Why?"

His eyes grew wide. "God is with that child. I saw the whole thing. There's no way he should be alive after what happened to him! When the car hit him, he flew about fifty feet through the air before smacking headfirst into the ground. I thought for sure he was dead. Now, here he is walking around today. A *true* miracle!"

He was absolutely right. I was indeed an amazing, walking miracle. Yet I still had miles of hell to crawl through before that miracle could truly save me.

## Chapter Two

I was in Stockton for a year when the string of my yo-yo life jerked me back up to Seattle. Grandma decided it would be best to move back, because we could live with Uncle John again. She knew some folks there, too. Plus, I could visit my Mom in prison. So once again, I was on a Greyhound bus making the eight-hundred-mile trip up north. This time I was excited—I desperately wanted to see my Mom.

I was now six years old and it'd been almost two years to the day since I'd last seen my mother. Grandma and I got Uncle John to drive us the fifty miles south to the Purdy Women's Correctional Facility in Gig Harbor, where both Mom and Auntie Sherry were. When we arrived, it was nothing like they showed in the movies or on TV. I could see Mom was in some type of minimum-security prison. It looked a lot like a college campus because the women were wearing their own clothes instead of jumpsuits. While most kids mothers take them to places like McDonald's or a circus, I visited my mother's cell. It was about eight feet by six feet and there were pictures on the wall, a television, and a door instead of the sliding iron bars. Really, it was like a tiny, cozy little bedroom, not the concrete walls of cells I'd seen on TV. Even with all this, Mom said it wasn't a nice place and she couldn't wait to get home. I hugged her forever and didn't want to let her go because I missed her so deeply. I couldn't wait for her to come home either. For the next six months, that would be the only time I'd see her.

***

I was in first grade when a problem at school reared its ugly head. It would be a big test of my relationship with Grandma; one that would tell me how I really stood with her. It started with the fact that I was the only black kid in the entire school—a school located in the suburbs. My teacher was middle-aged and white. She had this long, curly, brown hair and thick glasses glued to her face that made her look sinister. To me, she was downright scary.

I had barely settled in to the class when right out of the gate she called on me to read aloud. I knew I could read just fine but because I was nervous, I stuttered a little bit. She seemed to enjoy it. From then on, she called on me all the time, much more than any of the white kids in the class. I could almost hear her thinking, "This little nigger boy is ignorant. He'll never be able to keep up. He just doesn't have the ability."

After a week of this harassment, she called home and told Grandma that I was not at the reading level I should be and that—as far as reading goes—I was far behind the rest of the class. My grandmother didn't believe her. She knew I could read just fine, at least for my age. When I came home the next day she asked, "What's going on in that class? Can't you read?"

I protested. "Yes! I can read just fine. You know I can. This teacher is just picking on me because I'm the only black kid in school. She calls on me way more than any other kid and I get nervous each time she does it. Really Grandma, you gotta believe me!"

"Alright boy, calm down. I'll take care of it."

Grandma called the teacher back and let her know she was confident I could read at the level I should be. She explained how she'd witnessed me reading many times and that I'd done well each time. The teacher told her to come in and see for herself how far behind I was.

The next day, in walked Grandma. My heart started beating so fast I thought I'd pass out.

"Class," the teacher said, "this is Roosevelt's grandmother. She's going to sit in class and observe us today."

Grandma found an empty desk at the very front of the room and moved it right next to the teacher's desk.

Now I was looking at both the teacher and Grandma. That was twice as frightening! After a few minutes of this, sure enough, I heard these words: "Roosevelt, why don't you read page twenty-six out loud."

Suddenly, I was more nervous than I'd ever been before. I knew that if I failed, they would send me to Special Ed and label me a dummy for the rest of my life. This was a big turning point in my young life.

I cleared my throat and tried to relax. I knew Grandma was here to represent me and that I had to get it together and nail this or she'd deal with me later. That wasn't something I wanted to face. Just as I was to begin reading, Grandma shifted her position in the chair and somehow her big purse fell over, spilling the contents everywhere. As the kids in the class laughed, I ran up front to help her get everything back into the purse. It was a nice break, which helped to loosen me up. A minute later, I was back at my desk, ready for my performance.

I drew in a deep breath and let it fly. Sure enough, I nailed it! I read every word without a glitch. Not a single stutter, hesitation, mispronunciation or anything. It was flawless. I continued past page twenty-six until I'd finished the entire chapter. When I was done, I looked up at Grandma, saw her wink, and smile as if to say, "Great job Rose!" I closed the book as she stood up, repositioning the desk back to the front row. Then she looked at the teacher, pointed her finger, and spat this out: "Just like I said, he reads perfectly fine. Now get off his back and stop picking on him! Don't call me no more." I watched her walk out and that was that. Had it not been for Grandma sticking up for me, I would've joined the multitude of little black kids who had their lives ruined because "They just don't have the brains of normal people." Sadly, that wasn't the end of it. I knew from then on that I couldn't afford to have a bad day without someone holding it against me. Everyone else could slip up, trip over their words, and make mistakes on tests. They'd be granted all the grace in the world. However, when it came to me, they amplified every little thing I did and deemed it unacceptable. This caused me to learn and perform at the highest levels of everything. I had to go beyond the call of duty in any situation and this would make me only as good as the next guy—the next white guy. Grandma continued watching over me, making sure I progressed in school.

Back at Uncle John's house, I tried to settle in and get used to the neighborhood, the one I'd left two years ago. Not all was bliss there, either. One day I was at the playground next to our house playing with a hula-hoop. I was just twirling it around my wrist, minding my own business. Before long, another boy came walking up to me from the other side of the playground. He appeared older than I did and he was definitely much bigger, especially since I was small for my age.

He said, "Hey, can I play with your hula-hoop?"

I looked at him and said, "Sure, you can have a turn with it." I handed him the hoop and he began twirling it around his wrist, his neck, and then his waist. After a few minutes, he started throwing it up in the air and running back and forth across the playground with it. I began to grow impatient as he was taking a long turn with my hula-hoop, so I said, "Hey, can I have it back now?"

He smirked and said, "Nope!"

Confused, I said, "No seriously, it's time for me to go home. I need my hula-hoop."

He laughed and said, "That's too bad, it's mine now."

Just then, I noticed my Uncle Junior walking up the street. He was my mom's younger brother and had recently moved to Seattle to join the rest of the family. I ran over and told him what this kid had done. Uncle Junior said, "Okay, let's go get it back." We walked to the playground where the kid was still twirling away. Uncle Junior leaned over and whispered in my ear, "Kick him in his stomach and snatch the hula-hoop away. Go!"

I took off towards the kid and with all the force I could muster, I planted a shoe right in his gut. As he doubled over to the ground and gasped for air, I snatched my hula-hoop from his cold hands. The kid struggled to his feet and stood there crying. Wearing a smile of victory, I looked back at Uncle Junior, but he wasn't satisfied and yelled out, "Now finish him off!"

I knew exactly what he meant. I began to rain blows down on his head, completely thrashing this bully. Apparently, the kid wasn't ready for all this and didn't put up any defense. When I was almost spent, I pushed him backwards as hard as I could into a large bush, which caused him to cry even harder. Seeing him lying there, weak and helpless satisfied me. I turned to Uncle Junior, slapped my hands clean, and said, "That's good."

He said, "Okay Rose, let's go."

We went back to the house and said nothing. Uncle Junior never told anyone and we never spoke of it again, but from that day forward, I knew I'd never let anyone take anything from me ever again.

*** 

By May of 1980, Mom and Auntie Sherry came home from prison but we all still spent a lot of time at my Grandma's house. At that time the Dukes of Hazard were very popular and I watched them every chance I got. At a garage sale a few doors down from our house, a lady had a cool Dukes of Hazard lunch box just sitting there waiting for some lucky kid to claim it. I decided that I was that kid. The problem was, I didn't have their asking price—fifty cents.

When I got back to the house, Grandma, Mom and Auntie Sherry were all sitting there. I asked Grandma for the fifty cents and she gave it to me, but by the time I made it back to the garage sale, they'd already shut it down and gone inside. Since it was a Saturday, I assumed they'd be reopening the next day so I tucked away my money and waited.

Early the next morning, I awoke and ran down to their house, but only made it halfway. Standing there in the street all by myself, I stared up at a giant mushroom cloud. I thought, "What is this?" I'd never seen anything like it before. There was an eerie feeling all around. I just stood there for what was probably several minutes. Then I heard a noise in front of me and saw the family setting out items for the garage sale. When they saw me looking over their roof, they turned around to see what I was finding so fascinating. Instantly they ran back inside and grabbed their camera. They stood in the street snapping photos and I asked, "What is it?"

The man said, "Mount St. Helens has erupted!"

"Huh?" I said.

"Mount St. Helens has erupted! It's a volcano man...it just blew up!"

It turned out that Mount St. Helens had been showing some signs of volcanic activity and this was expected. However, at such a young age, I wasn't much for watching the news. I had no idea that Mount St. Helens even existed. Although this event was completely captivating, I still wanted my Dukes of Hazard lunch box. Before I could run home and tell my family, I said to the guy, "Here's my fifty cents for the Dukes of Hazard lunch box. Can I just grab it from the table?"

I placed the two quarters in his palm and he muttered "Okay," still transfixed on the large cloud. With my lunch box in hand, I rushed back home and found everyone still rubbing the sleep out of their eyes. "Hey everybody," I yelled. "Come look outside. Mount St. Helens erupted and you can see it in the sky!"

Auntie Sherry said, "Boy shut up! Ain't no Mount St. Helens erupted!"

I shook my head vigorously. "Yes it did, just come and see."

They stared at me trying to determine if I was lying. Auntie Sherry said, "Boy, If I come out there and you're lying, your ass is gonna be sore. Understand?"

"Okay, just come on out."

Seeing that I knew I'd get a whipping if I were lying, they decided to risk it. Tightening their robes, they made their way outside. When they did, they stood transfixed as I had. The next morning, even though we were over 180 miles away, there was a solid layer of ash covering everything just as if it had rained gray snow. The vision of this volcano blowing was both shocking and awesome. It was also devastating to the community nearest to it—fifty-seven people died and the landscape was forever changed. I remember sitting on the front porch steps wondering how Pops felt locked up inside a prison, knowing if he had to, he couldn't run from it.

\*\*\*

After a while things got back to normal but prison had changed Mom. She was tougher, meaner somehow. She didn't take any mess, especially from me. She demanded respect and wouldn't hesitate to slap me in the face to get it. One time I was in the store and some white kid was flipping out, crying about something he wanted. Mom grabbed me by the arm and said, "You see how that kid's acting? If you ever act like that, I will beat you in front of everybody. You hear me?"

I swallowed hard. "Yes ma'am."

Before we walked into a store, she'd jerk me aside and say, "Don't touch nothing. Don't look at nothing. Don't ask for nothing, because you ain't getting nothing. And if you do, I'll handle my business right in front of everybody, so everybody can see." I would nod my head and give no fuss—I fully believed her. That's just how black mommas got down back then. They used fear to keep kids in line. They knew once a kid got out of line, they'd lost control and it would be very hard to get it back.

By the time I turned ten, I was officially a latchkey kid. I would come home from school to an empty apartment and wait for Mom to get home from work. Pops was still in prison with no real date for release and Mom was working a full-time job taking all the overtime she could get. This happened for so long that I became independent and learned to do things for myself. I could cook my own meals and clean the house. I was also able to ride the city bus all over town. Like it or not, I was growing up fast.

The summer before I turned eleven, Mom was working a lot, so to save time she let me do my own shopping for new school clothes. She put $300 in my hand and said, "Don't let me down." I didn't. I took the city bus to the mall on the other side of town and successfully purchased all of my school clothes. As an adult I realized that I was too young to be doing such things, but at the time I was competent and it seemed normal.

When school started in the fall, I was in the fifth grade, one of only two black kids attending Wildwood Elementary School. I had a white friend named Timmy Green and one day, just as we heard the bell clanging an end to recess, we found ourselves at the furthest end of the soccer field. We knew we'd be in trouble for being late, so we started running towards the classrooms. I was just ahead of Timmy and for reasons still unknown to me, Timmy came up from behind, kicked out his foot, and tripped me. As I fell face first and hit the dirt, he jumped on my back and had my arms pinned down with his knees.

I said "What the hell are you doing?! Get off of me!"

Timmy said, "You're a weak little *nigger*. Look at you. You can't even get up and I can pretty much do whatever I want to."

I spit out, "Well you'd better keep me here forever cuz' when I get up, I'm gone show you how weak I am!"

He laughed and kept me pinned down so I couldn't move. Eventually, he said, "I've already proved I'm stronger than you, so I'm gonna let you up. Now, you're gonna behave, right?"

I calmed down and said, "Okay, man. Just let me up."

He let me up and we started walking to class, but this time, I let him get a little ahead of me. Inside I was so furious that I was seeing red. I thought to myself, "There's no way I'm letting him get away with this." The more I thought about it, the more enraged I became. Finally, I called out to him.

"Hey, bitch, turn around!"

As he turned his face to me, I threw a punch packed with the force of my entire body weight. My fist cracked him right in the mouth, exploding his top lip into a cascade of blood. The large gap between his two front teeth made the tear even wider. I looked around and blood was everywhere. He began to fall backwards, caught himself, and instead of fighting back, started crying and running to the front office. Of course, they didn't care to hear some black kid's story about why I'd done what I did. They just suspended me. When I got home, I told Mom exactly what he'd done to me and that he'd called me a nigger.
She licked her lips and thought about it. Then she said, "You know, he got what he deserved."

Timmy ended up with twelve stitches in his top lip and a scar to look at in the mirror for the rest of his life. I hoped it'd be something to remind him of me, make him think twice before he messed with another 'nigger.'
A couple weeks later, Mom told me we were moving fifty miles south to Tacoma. In the ten young years of my life, I'd moved four times already and there'd be many more moves before I turned eighteen.

## *Chapter Three*

I was once again a stranger in a strange town.
Leaving friends behind is always hard and it never got
any easier no matter how many times I did it. On top of
that, I always left my reputation behind, which meant
no one knew if I was a weakling or a tough guy. That
meant kids would spend some time getting to know me
before deciding on whether or not to bully me. That's
why it wasn't long before I ran into problems. This
time it all started over a girl.

We moved into an apartment complex and I quickly
fell for a cutie two courtyards over. We would run into
each other at the playground where she was always
nice to me and almost flirtatious, if you could call it
that between ten year olds. I'd heard a rumor there was
some thirteen-year-old boyfriend lurking in the
shadows but to date, I'd never seen this guy. So
eventually, I chose to believe the rumor wasn't true
and that I actually had a chance.

One day after we'd finished running around the playground, I put my arm around her and walked her home. She never removed it or told me to stop. In fact, we were both having a good time and enjoying each other's company. Once we'd gotten to her apartment and she'd gone inside, I started walking back home. I was about halfway when one of the neighborhood kids ran up to me and said, "I saw you with your arm around her. I'm gonna tell her boyfriend and he's gonna beat you up!"

Now I'm not going to lie—I was nervous. However, I also knew I couldn't let him see it. I puffed out my chest and said, "So what! Am I supposed to be scared?" He started running away from me and shouting, "I would be if I was you!" My nervous bucket immediately filled up.

The next day rolled around and as usual, I was home alone. There was still an hour left before Mom came home so when I heard a knock at the door, I looked through the peephole intent on not opening up the door for anyone. Once I got a good, clear view, I saw the same kid from yesterday, the one who'd said he'd tell on me. He seemed to be alone, so I opened the door and said, "Hey, what's up?"

Suddenly, a large monster of a kid jumped in front of me and stood there huffing and puffing like a psychopath. A thrill of sheer terror raced through my entire body. On reflex, I went to slam the door, thinking to myself, "Damn, the rumor is true! I'm a dead man." The kid reached the doorway before I could get it shut and forced the door back open. Once inside, he pushed me into the apartment and onto the ground where he wrapped his meaty hands around my neck as if he were going to choke me, but he wasn't squeezing hard. Then he angrily said, "Stay away from my girlfriend or I'll kill you!" With that, he let go and ran away.

I lay there trying to sort everything out. It appeared I was okay. There were no broken bones or necks. Nothing hurt except my pride. I was angry, but I was even more embarrassed. Once I'd crawled back to my feet, I closed and locked the door and then called my mother to tell her what had just happened. She was livid and said she'd deal with it when she got home. An hour later she clomped up the stairs with her youngest sister in tow —my Auntie Rachel. Grabbing my wrist she said, "Come on, let's go find him!" Against my vigorous protests, we got in the car and started driving around. I used this opportunity to beg them to turn around, explaining how this kid was a giant—an ogre. I wanted no part of this man-child— he'd implanted fear in me. Lots of it. I figured they were about to do what Uncle Junior had made me do: stand up to him. If they did, I was a goner.

As our car circled around, I prayed we didn't see him, but when Mom pulled around one of the buildings, there was a group of kids huddled together. Mom pulled right up in front of them and said, "Is one of those kids him?"

Reluctantly, I pointed the would-be killer out. "That's him right there."

I was certain now that she saw how big this beast was she'd have mercy on me but nope. She parked and said, "When we get out, you jump on him and whoop his ass. And you'd better not lose or you're gonna have to deal with me!"

Truthfully, I was already defeated—I simply couldn't imagine beating someone so much bigger than me. I had to go for it anyway, because I was honestly more afraid of what Mom would do if I didn't. I reluctantly got out of the car, went up to him, and gave him a shove. It barely moved him. Then, after a split second of curiosity, he charged at me. To my surprise, just before his body collided with mine, Auntie Rachel stepped over and slapped him across the face so hard that everybody standing there could feel it. He stopped his charge, stood there stunned, and then began blubbering like a baby right in front of everybody.

It was surreal. He simply staggered off rubbing his cheek and crying for his momma while somehow, I was unhurt. It wasn't a physical win for me, but I learned once again not to be afraid of a bully. I needed to stand my ground and fight.

The more I thought about it, the more I realized it was always better to stand and fight no matter what the outcome, than to be a punk and run away. I know I could've resented my mother for this. Her parenting in condoning violence was unfit, dysfunctional, and abusive. Instead of complaining, I tucked away that valuable lesson for later, one I still hold today.

***

Mom had landed a job as an office assistant at a small office building and began working on the manager to let me work at cleaning the building. Finally, he agreed. My job was to sweep the sidewalk, pick up trash around the building, and keep the restrooms clean. I worked on Tuesdays and Thursdays for about an hour and I was paid $10 a week. Since I had to pass the office building every day when I walked home from school, it was easy to just stop in and do the job.

I'd been working for about a month when Mom learned Pops was moving to a different prison. The place he was in now—Walla Walla State Penitentiary—was a full 260 miles away. Being so far away, I hadn't visited him much. The last time I'd seen him was a couple of years ago. Now I was ten and learned he'd only be thirty minutes away at McNeil Island Prison (which was Washington's version of Alcatraz). Of course, both were extremely nasty, harsh places, but now I could see my father more.

Mom had known that with only two years left on his sentence, he would eventually move closer to home. That's why we moved to Tacoma—so we could visit him more. The first time we planned to visit Pops, I cleaned up real nice and brushed out my clothes. I wanted to look my best. When I was done, I watched Mom sit at the kitchen table rolling marijuana up tightly into a plastic baggie. When it was good and tight, she slipped a balloon over it and tied it into a tight knot. That much she didn't mind me witnessing. Just before she shoved the entire package up her vagina, she went into the bathroom and closed the door.

When we were ready, we took the drive to Steilacoom to catch the ferry to McNeil Island. Once there, we walked up the long pier to the prison where guards thoroughly searched both of us before they admitted us to the visiting room. While we waited for Pops to appear, Mom went to the bathroom and came carefully shifting the marijuana around in her pockets. That's when I realized she had gone to the bathroom and removed it from her vagina. Because we had contact visits, Mom slipped it into her hand so when they hugged, Pops pulled it away in his. Where he put it to avoid detection from the guards, I didn't ask.

This went on every visit without fail, until one day they were finally able to get married. Up until this point, they'd never tied the knot (not counting the one on the marijuana-filled balloon). Once they found a preacher in the prison who would marry them, Mom mailed Pops a white suit to wear. On the day of their wedding, Mom prepared the weed like normal except this time she dressed in something very nice. When we cleared inspections and Mom had gone to the bathroom, guards escorted us to the prison chapel instead of the visiting room. I looked around and there was Mom, Pops, a preacher, two prison guards, and me. Everyone greeted each other and we all stood in this tiny concrete room with no windows and a door full of iron bars. The preacher conducted the ceremony, my parents exchanged vows, and then they were pronounced husband and wife. That was it. There was no music, no confetti, no reception, no cake, no gifts, and no honeymoon. They had a few words with the preacher before we returned to the regular visiting room where we visited for a couple of hours, slipped the weed into Pops' hands, and went home.

For the next several days, Mom frantically searched through the mail waiting for some notice. When it finally arrived, she jumped up and down. This was her notice that the prison approved conjugal visits, since Pops was behaving. One Saturday morning, Mom woke me up early and loaded up some groceries, packed some clothes in a bag, sprayed on some perfume, wrapped up the weed and stuffed it in its usual place, and we were off to the prison. This time the guards let us walk to an area with two small mobile homes enclosed with tall barbed wire fences. There was also a worn out playground in front of the trailers. Mom told me we would be staying with Pops until Sunday afternoon. I soon learned this meant I sat outside in the playground with the kids from the other trailer while moans and groans drifted out from the trailers as they rocked back and forth. This went on for hours. Occasionally I'd smell the weed Mom had brought with her. It was amazing. The prison system allowed conjugal visits to assist inmates in their transition back into society by giving them the opportunity to spend some time in a 'home-like' environment. Having sex and smoking weed all day was actually going to help my father get right back into the swing of things, since that's what he was planning on doing once he was free.

\*\*\*

Mom ended up befriending the preacher who'd married them, Reverend Jackson. He offered to let us stay rent-free in one of his rental houses. The house itself was barely habitable and smelled like a damp, moldy building. There was no furniture at all on the first floor, just an old table with two chairs in the kitchen. Upstairs in Mom's room was a mattress on the floor and a TV. In my room, there was only a mattress on the floor. It reminded me of the Norman Bates *Psycho* house, the one I'd seen in the movie.

One morning as I woke up and stretched to the ceiling, I heard Mom calling from downstairs, "Oh my God! Roosevelt! Come down here!"

I jumped up and ran halfway down the stairs, stopping midway to look at the living room floor. I couldn't believe what I was seeing. We didn't have a trashcan in the kitchen so we used a large paper grocery bag. There was the trash strewn across the entire kitchen *and* living room floor with the actual bag now sitting next to front door. It looked as if a large animal had been inside and trashed the place. The loaf of bread that was sitting on the kitchen counter had a large tunnel through the entire loaf, from end to end. It didn't take long to figure out there was a *serious* rat problem. Mom talked to Rev. Jackson and he gave her only one trap, which she promptly handed to me and said it was my responsibility to set it. I was so little and the trap was so big—about as long as my entire arm—one false move and 'Snap!' I could've lost a hand just like that. I was super careful as I used all my strength to force back the clamp and set the pin to keep it in place.

The first morning after I had set the trap, I awoke to find a rat in it no less than a foot long, not including the tail. Its face was hideous, as if it had screamed out in pain right before it died. Its sharp, jagged teeth made me glad I was running into this creature while it was dead. I took the trap outside and emptied the rat into the trash, resetting it before we went to bed that night. Sure enough the next morning there was another foot long rat in the trap just waiting for me. A week into this we figured out there was no shortage of these ugly beasts. They must have sent out the message that there was food for the taking and flooded our home with their kin. Each one died with that hideous scowl on their face like it was cursing me. It didn't take long for us to learn rent-free was not *rat-free*.

I turned eleven still living in this rat-hole and made friends with Rev. Jackson's son Willie. He was the same age as me, so I would go down to his house after school and hang out. There was this kid Frankie who lived across the street from the Jacksons. He was a couple years older and was always bullying and pushing us around. If we were outside, he messed with us. If we were inside, he just came inside, too. Since we were all latchkey kids, we were powerless to stop him. It didn't take long for him to own us. One day we were hanging out in Willie's kitchen, getting something to drink before we went back outside to play. Apparently Frankie had designated today as 'Pick on little Roosevelt day,' he came in the back door and helped himself to a drink while bumping and elbowing me several times. I could tell he was hoping I'd react. If I showed any emotion whatsoever, he'd shove me in the back of the head and then tease me by making jokes about my height. After that, he'd poke his finger into my chest and keep on taunting me. This guy stood over a foot taller than me, and although I was completely terrified of him, I was getting angrier by the minute. I imagined myself taking a swing and knocking him out cold. Still, he continued to taunt me and I did nothing about it.

While we all stood in the kitchen, I waited for Willie
to say something in my defense or make him stop, but
Willie just stood idly by. I could tell he was just as
afraid of Frankie as I was. Finally, I reached my boiling
point and snapped. I looked over and noticed a wooden
closet rod. It was an inch-and-a-half in diameter and
as long as I was tall. It seemed to be leaning against the
wall just waiting for something to do. I knew I was just
the one it'd been waiting for.

I snatched it up and pulled it back before bringing it
forward in a wide arc. Frankie lifted his head at the
whistling sound it made slicing through the air, but
didn't know where it was coming from until it was too
late. The solid wooden rod made a sick sound as it both
smacked and crunched his face, knocking him to the
floor. I drew the rod back feeling the beast inside me
rage. It wanted out and so I unlocked the cage. The
whistling sound once again signaled a blow was
coming, but this time Frankie used his arms to cover
his head and began yelling for me to stop. Yet it was
too late—the beast was now loose and out of control.

The rod hit him again in the head. He crumpled closer to the ground screaming in pain, but it was no use. The beast in me hit him again and again. There were blows on his arms, legs, and back. No area was off limits. The beast fully remembered the bully who took my hula-hoop.

*Whack!*

And the bully who told me to leave his girl alone.

*Whack!*

And Timmy for pinning me to the ground and calling me nigger.

*Whack!*

The beast wanted to hurt him so bad that he could never look at me again. And the beast wanted blood and broken bones. God only knows how many blows rained down before the beast took a deep breath and was satisfied, crawling back into his cage for another day. When I opened my eyes, I saw a bruised and bleeding Frankie curled up in a fetal position, crying and helpless. I looked over at Willie and he was speechless, a look of total shock spread across his face. Incredibly, even though Frankie was hurt pretty badly, nothing was broken. From that day forward, he never teased, taunted, or laid a finger on me—ever again. In fact, whenever I saw him, he had a completely different attitude. I honestly think I cured him of being a bully.

A few days later, Willie and I walked a mile to the fish market where we often hung out. Bullies picked on Willie a lot, because no one had ever taught him to fight back. His dad, being a preacher, taught Willie peace and to turn the other cheek. As a result, bullies constantly hit Willie's cheeks. It was pretty sad.

I remember us sitting there on a stone wall, talking about our lives. He spoke about running and hiding from the bullies while I confessed to him that I didn't see my life getting any better. I told him I woke up each day with a father in prison and to a mother who put weed up inside her to smuggle into him, knowing if she got caught they would both do more time and leave me with no parents again. I cleaned out a rattrap each morning with another monster staring at me. I had an endless supply of bullies who wanted to beat me up too. We also lived in poverty so crushing, Mom and I slept on the floor and waited for the rats to figure out that they could simply bypass the food and come straight to us and take a hunk of warm, bloody flesh.

That's why I slept each night curled tightly in blankets: I was imagining I heard the little rat feet coming after me. It was awful.
I turned to Willie and said, "You know, my life's a shithole. Really, there's no way I'm gonna crawl out of this and make something of myself." Then I saw a bucket of crabs at the fisherman's stall and tapped Willie on the arm. "Come here," I said.

Pointing into the bucket, I said, "My life's like this bucket of crabs. See that crab on top? He's almost to the edge of the bucket but the other crabs pull him back down. Then one of them gets on top and they all pull him back down. That's what my life's like—a bucket of crabs. Everyone in this shitty bucket just keeps pulling each other down, making sure no one ever escapes. That right there," I said, my finger almost touching the top crab, "is my life. It's all I have to look forward to." Then, I glanced around to make sure no one was looking and kicked the bucket over, freeing the crabs from their hellhole and running hard before I got caught.

## *Chapter Four*

The $10 I made each week was nice, but I wanted more money to buy stuff, things kids my age were wearing. Mom was barely able to put food on the table and a roof over our heads, so she certainly didn't have any extra money for me. When she did have extra money, it went straight to the baggies of weed she smuggled into prison. That meant I was on my own. I started looking around for extra work and soon heard about this group called Teens in Action. Several kids my age were doing it and making some money. I decided to check it out.

This middle-aged white man, Beauregard, ran it. He wore plaid shorts—the kind that were cut off from dress slacks—and black socks that failed to cover his pasty white legs. Black dress shoes, a white t-shirt and thick prison glasses filled out the rest of his look. He drove a white panel van with no windows and the whole thing would've made sense if he'd stopped in the neighborhoods tempting little kiddies with candy into his van while holding a video cam. Instead, he dropped off black kids like me in upper class neighborhoods with a script to perform at each front door.

"Hello ma'am, my name is Roosevelt and I'm here today with Teens in Action. Teens in Action is a youth organization designed to keep young men like myself off the streets and out of trouble. I'm hoping you would help me out today by taking a look at some of our items."

Our items were boxes of candy. We sold them for $4 apiece and he bought them for 50¢. We kept $1 and the rest went to Beauregard for "spenses" as he called them. To help with sales, Beauregard turned our ball caps slightly off center and sometimes he smudged dirt on us to make us look young, poor, and hungry. He also trained us to be sympathetic, almost shy. It worked. Each time I hit the streets I made $10 to $12. When we had finished walking our territory, we met up at a designated street corner and he came along with his van and picked us up to go to a new neighborhood. It was a slick operation. Did I say it was for a good cause?

Now that I had some dough in my pocket, I started fitting in more. My first two purchases were shell-toe Adidas shoes which I wore with no laces and a Kangol bucket hat. It wasn't long before I added sunglass frames without the glass, which we called 'school boys.' Hip-hop was still new, fresh, and exciting. Back then, you would rarely hear obscene lyrics or anything close to the explicit content that's in today's music. With this new genre of music, I finally found a culture that identified with me personally. The music spoke directly to me, and people who looked and spoke just like me were the artists behind it. I felt my identity validated by the popularity of the hip-hop crowd.

Almost overnight, folks in my neighborhood dove into the music. There were boom boxes propped up on shoulders everywhere I looked. They were cranked up so loud that the sounds of break beats and rap songs blared constantly through the streets. It was all about the music, fashion, graffiti street art, and break dancing. If there was a disagreement between crews, we settled it on the cardboard in a b-boy battle. Very rarely, if ever, did it escalate to violence. For me this was a magical time; it gave me hope I might actually climb out of my bucket of crabs.

With the new, trendy Roosevelt now walking the streets of the hood, I began turning my attention to the ladies. Well, actually to young girls. I loved the feeling I'd get when I flirted with the pretty girls at school. When I came up on a phone number, it felt like a huge accomplishment. I'd stay on the telephone for hours talking to a cutie, and sometimes all night. Back then, there were no flat rates for phone service, so I got plenty of complaints from Mom about the large phone bill. Then, if I happened to get a brief peck on the lips, it was the greatest thing I'd ever felt; it always gave me a severe case of puppy love. I must have fallen in love at least a hundred times. With love like that, I almost forgot the bullies. Almost.

I was in the seventh grade at Jason Lee Junior High when I turned twelve. Of course, there had to be trouble there, and this time trouble was named Donald Tanner. Donald was a very popular ninth grader. He was also an amateur Golden Gloves boxer. I soon found out that very much like Frankie, Donald was a bully who liked to pick on little guys like me. My body size made me an easy target. Every day Donald would throw rocks at me and tease me about being short. One day, after I had had enough of this punk, I told Donald, "If you don't leave me alone, I'm gonna get my big brother to kick your ass!" Lavon was my half-brother through my father and had just started living with us. He'd lived with his mother until she was brutally beaten to death in a Las Vegas motel room several years ago. He'd then become a ward of California, bouncing around in foster homes where he had also learned to protect himself through fighting. Lavon was a bad ass—a human lethal weapon—and as far as I was concerned, nobody could beat him.

When Donald heard my threat, he tossed his head back and laughed. "I ain't worried about you, Shortie. I'll get my little brother to whip you!"

I swallowed hard. His little brother was Shawn Tanner and also an amateur Golden Gloves boxer. These guys knew how to handle themselves, because all they did was fight. But I'd learned that no matter how afraid I was, I couldn't show fear or I'd be dead. Guys like Donald feasted on scared prey.

I took a deep breath and said, "I ain't worried about your little brother!" Then I turned and walked away. When I got home, I decided not to get Lavon involved, mainly because I wanted this to die down. It worked— for about a week. Then one day I was standing in the gym after school talking to Karrie, a girl I was trying to get to know. Things were looking good until she looked over my shoulder. Her eyes widened and her mouth opened, and seeing that expression, I turned around and saw Shawn Tanner stomping over. As I watched him move closer, it was as if everything was in slow motion. My heart dropped to my feet and my hands began to sweat. I was scared as hell, but I knew there was no way to back down—not in front of a girl or my peers at school.

Shawn barked out, "I hear you been saying you could whoop me. What's up?"

I said, "Man, don't come up to my school like you some tough shit homie!"

Shawn smiled and nodded. "Let's go outside and handle it then."

"Let's do it!" I said.

We walked outside and it seemed like the whole school was following us. I knew there was no way I could win this fight. Still, I couldn't show my fear so I just committed myself mentally to get it over with and do the best I could.

We stopped outside the school gym and rolled up our sleeves. Then we squared off against each other, surrounded by a circle of kids who were both cheering and egging us on. He threw the first punch, which I ducked. As I lowered my head, I countered with a right that connected to his jaw. He stepped back, shook it off and continued throwing punches, landing a few glancing blows on the side of my head. We exchanged a few blows until I saw a chance to hit him again in the same spot on the jaw. The second it connected, he fell to the ground completely dazed. That's when I heard my Uncle Junior's voice ringing in my ears, "Now finish him off Rose!" I saw a skateboard on the ground and picked it up raising it high above my head. This would likely kill him but I didn't care. The beast was loose and out of control.

I swung the skateboard down towards his skull when suddenly my friend James Willard tackled me. He yelled into my face, "No man. That's enough!" James was twice my size and he lifted me up in the air and rushed me away from the scene yelling, "It's over man, you won! You won! But you almost took it too far." I didn't realize then but James not only saved Shawn's life, but mine as well.

The next day at school, the principal called me to his office. I sat facing this ancient man while he told me that he was going to act as if this never happened because Shawn didn't belong on the campus and wasn't a student here. Then he told me I'd better not have any more problems with fighting. I nodded and left his office, thankful he didn't suspend me again. The funny thing was, I never had a problem with either Donald or Shawn again.

With that crisis behind me, I went to school each day with my favorite hip-hop tapes in my pocket, (Run DMC, Kurtis Blow, Whodini, U.T.F.O., The Fat Boys) and a Walkman on my hip. During breaks, I'd slip on my headphones and rap to the music, really feeling like I was living the high life. My two jobs were putting about $50 a week in my pocket, which was big money to me. Really, I was starting to see daylight at the end of the long rat tunnel.

***

At the far end of my apartment complex lived Andre, a twelve-year-old latchkey kid like me. We were good friends, and depending on our moods, we would hang out at his place or mine. Right next to Andre's apartment, lived a seventeen-year-old girl. We'd holler out immature remarks like, "Hey baby," and "I like what I see," every time she walked past. One day she stopped, looked at us, and said, "You young boys wouldn't even know what to do with a woman like me!" Of course, we said, "Yes we would!" We knew nothing would ever come of it.

She smiled back and said, "Okay, my mom works nights. If you ain't scared, come to my place tonight." When she left, Andre and I went into his apartment and discussed the matter. We were nervous, if we didn't show up, we'd be hearing about it from her forever and probably from some of our homies as well. Andre said, "Okay, Rose, let's at least show up and see what happens."

"Yeah, that's a good idea." I said. "We can always leave."

Later that night we showed up at her apartment and knocked on the door. She opened it up and said, "So I guess you boys are gonna show me how it's done, huh?"

I tried to lick my lips, but my mouth was bone dry. Neither of us said a word because we were so nervous. I started thinking about leaving the moment the door closed behind us. Then I felt her hand clasp my fingers and she led me to her bedroom. When she closed the door, I just stood there waiting to see what she would do next.

Then she began to drop her clothes to the floor. That's when my nervousness turned to arousal and my heart began racing, literally trying to burst from my chest. I thought, "Damn! This is really gonna happen!" It was something boys my age only dream about, but now it was about to go down for real. When I saw her naked bangin' body, I became paralyzed. I couldn't take my eyes off all the goodies.

Her skin was a smooth, creamy milk chocolate color with curves in all the right places. Still paralyzed, I had no idea what to do next. Seeing this, she took my twitching hands and placed them on her body, starting with her breasts, before moving them to her booty, and eventually ending up between her legs. The fabric of my shirt was thumping in and out trying to hold my heart in. My nervousness threatened to cut off the blood and oxygen to my brain and I was scared I might actually pass out. But because I was seeing the forbidden treasures—diamonds and gold I'd only dreamed about—I stayed conscious, although barely. Now she pushed me back on the bed and got on top of me with her long smooth legs tight against my hips. Button by button she removed my shirt, then the belt. Once that was off, she unzipped me and slid my pants and underwear off. I thought I might lose it right there, but before I could fully understand this fantasy, she pushed me inside her for a thirty-second euphoric ride. When I exploded, the light in my eyes exploded, too. It felt like my brain blasted into bits all over the walls. I held on to her waist while she rode me for a few minutes more, giving me time to catch my breath and regain consciousness. When she was done, she helped me get dressed since I was mostly unable. Then, in my foggy haze, she led me to the couch where I plopped down and was hardly aware she was taking Andre in there for his ride.

I blinked several times and told myself I was now a man. The experience was so addictive that we came back for the same routine several nights a week for a very long time. Hers was a body I couldn't get out of my mind. Now I understood a lot of things.

*** 

When you're twelve years old and your mother doesn't get home until after six and your father's in prison, it's easy to find trouble. One Saturday when I didn't have to work with Teens in Action, I hopped a bus with two friends and went to the mall. This was something we liked doing, since we each had money and usually we could hang out with other kids. We walked the mall looking for new clothes, yet finding nothing until we walked into Bon Marche.

Browsing through the racks, we spied these cool Adidas sweat suits, the kind that Run DMC wore. We decided to try them on so we took them to the dressing area and they looked real fly on us—yeah, we were fresh. Then we looked at the price tag and couldn't believe how expensive they were. Certainly none of us could afford them. That's when we got an idea. Why not just steal them?

I thought about it. Why not? It's probably what my Pops woulda done, so I went for it.
We carefully put our original clothes back over these dope ass sweat suits and walked out of the dressing room like nobody's business. We continued towards the exit, casually stopping to check out an item here and there before moving on. When we made it to the large opening that led into the mall, we were home free. But the second we stepped over the line it felt like a small army had surrounded us grabbing our arms and yanking us back inside the store.

In no time, we found ourselves in a small office. We sat down and they took our information. It wasn't long before Mom came busting in with a 'you're-so-dead' face. I hung my head as she grabbed my arm and it felt like she was trying to touch her thumb with her forefinger through my muscle. As I endured the pain, she led me to the car where she mapped out a horror movie type beating in her mind. When we got back to the apartment, she put her plan in action. Though I never faced criminal charges, I got it bad. Real bad. It was something I never forgot.

***

It was almost summer when Mom sat us down at the kitchen table and told us Pops was coming home in a few days. I thought of everything wrong he'd done, and how he'd been in prison so long. Instantly the bad feelings vanished. I wanted him back worse than anything I could imagine. Most of my friends didn't have fathers at home, so I knew when he got home, it would be like having something special. By the time we got him back to the apartment, I'd decided he could do no wrong.

It had been just Mom and me for so many years now. Now, we had Lavon and Pops and instantly we were a family, one that I was determined would be happy. And everything was just beautiful in the beginning. Mom and Pops were in love and always happy. Mom went to work while Pops was out each day looking for a job. Lavon and I were in school and all was going well. Even the bullies left me alone. At night, Pops sat around the living room keeping us laughing with his jokes. It just seemed like we were always happier when he was around. Sure, I knew all about his past: that he had hurt many people and was somewhat of a gangster back in the day, but none of that mattered to me now. I was proud to call him my father. Since he had no moral compass, all the bad things my brother and I wanted to do—things most parents wouldn't condone—he didn't have a problem with those things. It was great!

Then things started to slip, nothing big at first. I noticed he would ease out at night and leave Mom behind. In the beginning, she acted all happy, like it was part of the plan. Late at night, Lavon and I would hear him stagger in and then we'd fall asleep.

This began happening more and more, but at least he always came home. Until one night he didn't. I lay in bed tossing and turning trying to get to sleep as the minutes ticked by. The silence was deafening. I got up and went to the bathroom four times an hour thinking that somehow I'd heard him come in. And each time I discovered he wasn't home yet. Then the tiny clicks I was used to hearing as the apartment building settled continued fooling me into thinking Pops was putting his key into the lock and coming through the front door. And each time, nothing. No Pops.

The next morning, I saw the stress on Mom's face. Lavon had it too. Our protector, our king was leaving us behind to fend for ourselves. He was going back to the life he led before he went to prison. Just when we all thought we were crawling out of this pile of shit, something pulled us right back down into it.

## Chapter Five

Pops would come and go without saying much. Usually he'd be gone for long periods of time—like three or four days—before stumbling back home. I had no idea what he could've been doing all the time he was away, but I'll never forget the feelings of anxiety, worry and fear. I kept expecting someone to call and say they found him dead somewhere. And that wasn't unlikely— by now, it had happened to many of my friends' fathers. In fact, there were acres of graveyards filled with black fathers who never came home. But as for me, I didn't care about everyone else. I just wanted a father who was there for me.

Then one day I learned Pops had a mistress and her name was heroin. On the outside, he would look well-put together, sharply dressed, clean and neat, but in reality, he was a high-functioning dope fiend. Often times he'd say he was going to the store and would be right back, and then we wouldn't see him for days on end. Every time he did this, his family was home worried, no *terrified* for him when he was out on his binges, but that didn't change anything. Every night that he didn't come home was a sleepless night for me. My mom knew what was going on, but she never told me. I had to find out on my own. Knowing what Pops was up to didn't make it any easier on her. I could hear her in the next room awake and moving around. Sometimes I could hear her crying. Throughout the night, I'd get out of bed several times and look out my window to see if his car was in the driveway. It never was. In those days I thought for sure the only way a man doesn't come home to his family at night is when something terrible has happened to him. Those were the longest nights. My mind would punish me with a snowball of bad thoughts before turning into an avalanche of worst-case scenarios. Yet there were rare times when I saw his car parked outside, and then I'd feel the fear melt away. That's when I knew he's home, and we're all safe. Pulling the covers up tight to my neck, I could finally get some sleep.

With no father around to teach and guide me, I continued to race headlong down my own path. One street over was a run-down convenience store called Quickies, it was owned by a proud Jamaican couple. The first time I went in there, I was amazed. These two were true Rastafarians, complete with dreadlocks, reggae music, and the fragrance of incense everywhere. Just going in was an experience all to itself. With it being the only store close by, it wasn't long before I was going in there every day. Sometimes I was buying snacks for myself and other times for someone in my family. With Dad constantly missing, it was a nice diversion.

Usually the husband and wife ran the store, but occasionally the two daughters took care of things. The oldest, Amani, would handle the money and transactions at the counter. She was thirteen years old. Her younger sister, Althea, was ten and mostly just watched Amani. Of course, when I went there and saw the girls, I would flirt with them in a fun way, certainly not for any purpose. They would respond with giggles and smiles, acting as girls did at that age.

One day I gathered up my snacks and set them on the counter. As I dug into my pocket for the money, I noticed both girls were taking care of the store alone. Smiling at them and waiting for the total, Althea, the younger one said, "You don't have to pay."
Not sure I'd heard her right, I said, "Excuse me?"
Amani moved to the center of the counter and said, "She likes you. That's why whenever we're in here alone, you don't have to pay."

I was stunned. It was like winning the lottery. But even though I was still twelve, I had enough smarts to know I had to play along to keep this ATM paying. "That's perfect, because I like you too." Althea smiled and blushed as I gathered up my snacks and hurried out of the store before they changed their minds.

Over the next few weeks, I carefully watched Quickies and learned when the parents were gone. Each time I went there, I made a haul, paying only with a few smiles and my dazzling, twelve-year-old charm. After all, I came from a long line of charmers. (Between Pops and my two grandfathers, there were close to forty kids running around. That's a lot of charm!) One day, I suggested we exchange phone numbers to coordinate better the times that I could come to the store. They both agreed. Soon, I was waiting for the phone to ring so I could go and ring the money bell.

Now that I was talking to Althea on the phone a lot, I got to know more about her and especially her parents. She let it out that her parents didn't believe in using banks to put their money in. Instead, they kept stacks of cash sitting in a room in their house. Althea told me they had countless stacks of cash that reached the ceiling and they wouldn't even miss it if some of the money disappeared. I couldn't believe what I was hearing. I mean, could this get any better?

To test her, I said, "If they won't miss it, how about getting some for me?"

"No problem," she said. My heart was racing as we arranged a time to meet behind the store later that day.

When I showed up, she handed me a wad of cash. As payment, I gave her a kiss on the cheek and was quickly on my way. When I got back home, I counted the money. It was $75. I was so excited about this cute little Jamaican ATM; I wanted to tell someone about it. Then I thought I should be very careful. If I kept it to myself, I could have an endless supply of free cash. That was the smart play. Unfortunately, I was twelve so I *had* to tell my homeboy Demetri who lived across the street from Quickies.

When Demetri found out about the free bank, he approached Amani and bonded with her. Before you knew it, she was giving him money, too. Several times a week we were getting big wads of cash. One time Althea gave me $300 for the fictitious new bike I needed. When she handed the thick bankroll to me (mostly small bills), it looked like a million bucks. I ran home, pulled all this money out of my pocket, and threw it on the bed to show off to my brother Lavon. He was so shocked he let out a loud, "DAAAMN!" Pops just happened to be home and heard Lavon so he came in to see what the excitement was. I had to tell him what I'd been doing and where the money was coming from. As I said before, Pops had no moral compass, so he was cool with it. Then I wondered if he was going to plan a heist of the couple's place and steal all their cash, but Mom found out about it and threatened to go to Quickies and tell the parents what had been going on. Somehow, Pops talked her out of it and decided not to rob these people. This allowed me to continue getting cash except, this time, I didn't flaunt it around my mom. A couple of months later, their parents caught the girls taking the money and my Jamaican ATM was closed for good. But boy, what a great ride it was!

\*\*\*

We'd lived in Tacoma, Washington for three years when Mom decided to move back to Stockton, California. I don't know if Pops had any say in this, but he went along with it. I'd just turned thirteen and this would be my fifth move. Moving was always hard—I never knew when my friendships would be ripped apart. I was also realizing that any life I built was resting on sand and it would likely wash away at the next tidal shift in either of my parents' moods.

When we arrived back in Stockton, I quickly found a door-to-door job selling subscriptions to the Stockton Record Newspaper. It was the same deal as Teens in Action. We would get picked up by a creepy-looking guy in a van and go to different neighborhoods, except this time I was being paid $2.50 for every subscription and getting my money weekly. In no time, my highly polished "Would you like to help keep a teen off the streets by subscribing to a terrific newspaper?" was reeling in $80 a week. It wasn't as good as my Jamaican connection, but it was honest work—*mostly.*

Mom and Pops soon found work as professional writers. They would dress up in their good clothes, sit down at the kitchen table, take out nice pens, and begin writing. It never took them long to finish. With the forged checks in hand, they'd hop in the car and hit the town, looking for juicy banks and businesses to cash them. They were experienced at this so they knew the proper dollar limits and could avoid most of the problems. This meant more work, but hey, it kept them out of prison.

I soon found out there was a local boxing team for young boys and decided, after all the fights I'd been in, I wanted some of that. I joined up with two friends of mine who lived in the hood with me. The only problem was the distance: the gym was clear across town and my parents weren't going to take me. My friends were in the same boat. Then a solution presented itself.

There was a railroad track running right through our neighborhood (which for some reason is always present wherever poor folk live). Imagine that! To take advantage of this free transportation, I did one of the dumbest things ever: I jumped onto a moving train and rode it across town each day. That's right! My friends and I wanted to box so badly that we would run alongside a moving train, get close to a ladder, and then jump up, gripping onto the rungs. Slowly but surely we'd pull ourselves up and ride it eight miles before jumping off and tumbling hard along the ground. It was incredibly dangerous and one slip would likely throw us under the train, but we did it anyway. It was even more stupid when rain or a light mist was falling. This made it vital to grip hard. One time, though, my right hand slipped off, dragging the right side of my body along the tracks just like in the movies. With a great heave, I slung my body back onto the ladder and regained my grip, likely saving my life. Since it was too dark when practice ended to risk catching the train, we took the bus home.

I lasted at boxing for a few months and then realized it wasn't for me. I was a street brawler and found my moves in the streets didn't work at all in the ring. There was no way they'd allow me to pin someone's arms down to the mat with my knees while I pummeled their face and for sure they weren't gonna allow me to pick up a skateboard and bash in a skull. Nope. At least with no more boxing, I didn't have to risk my life running to catch that train every day.

The Saturday after I quit, the happening place to be was the mall. I was there with four of my buddies, messing around and playing video games at the arcade. We'd been there for about thirty minutes when I began looking for another game to play. Suddenly, I heard a kid yell out, "Get him, Rose! Get him, Rose!" Rose was what my friends called me, so that caught me off guard. I moved closer to the action and saw a kid playing Mortal Kombat surrounded by four other kids watching. They kept yelling, "Get him, Rose!" I stared hard at the kid and then moved on.

Later, while we were on our way home, my friends and I were at the back of the bus and sure enough, I saw this same kid again. His buddies were calling him Rose, just like in the arcade. Everybody was being loud and crazy so I just finally asked him, "Ay man, what's your name?"

He looked me up and down and said, "Roosevelt."
"Roosevelt?" I said. "My name's Roosevelt. So what's your last name?"
"Sargent."
Stunned, I said, "My last name's Sargent. What's your daddy's name?"
"June."
"What?! My daddy's name is June!" At that, everybody started cracking up and going crazy. No one could believe it. I thought I was having an out of body experience. When I finally regained my senses, I said, "Oh, you must be Tita."
"Yeah," he said. "We're brothers, homie. You don't know about me?"

We started comparing notes. I'd heard about him, but didn't know we both had the same name. It was bizarre meeting like this. Sometimes that's how it is in the hood, especially when a father spreads seeds everywhere. We talked the rest of the way home and exchanged phone numbers. Since that day, we've kept in touch.

I told Lavon about it and he was fascinated. He wanted to meet the kid but before we could, another incident happened. A week later Lavon and I were in a K-mart when I thought I saw Pops standing by the magazine rack. I stared and stared and was sure it was Pops, since he wore the same clothes and had the same stance. I tapped Lavon on the shoulder and said, "Look at that guy standing over there. He looks like our dad!" He squinted his eyes and stared hard. "Damn, he sure does! 'Cept he looks like Pops when he was younger." "Yeah, you're right." "C'mon, let's go over and meet him."

It turns out his name was Jalon Sargent. He was Pops' younger brother, another of our grandpa's unknown twenty-six seeds that he spread around before he died. It was just another crazy day in the life of Roosevelt Sargent—the real one! Ha ha, no offense, big bro!

***

A little while later, just as summer was ending, my parents discovered they'd just about drained all the good watering holes for hot checks in Stockton. It was time to move on. They also may have gotten wind of all the warrants out for their arrests. Regardless, Pops worked on Mom and convinced her Las Vegas was where they should be. He just knew they could hit it big there. So, we picked up and moved again. This time, though, Lavon didn't want to go so he decided to stay with one of our cousins in Stockton. I'm thinking maybe because his mom being murdered there had something to do with it. Anyway, the day before we left town, Mom took me on one final hot check blowout to let me stock up on new clothes for the coming school year. It sure felt good not having to sneak out the stolen goods under my clothes, and instead carry them out in store bags like proper thieves. It was just more dignified, more respectful.

The last few days Pops kept a very low profile, as I assumed the police were looking for him. When the wheels of our plane pulled up and we were high in the sky, Pops finally sat upright in his seat, acting like a king again, knowing that the extradition laws between states were tricky.

We landed in Vegas with only a few pieces of luggage each, having left everything else behind. My two bags were full of all my new clothes so I felt rich. The airport itself was thick with cigarette smoke and slot machines. The dings of coins dropping into the slots and bells from the machines echoing back and forth assaulted my ears. Occasionally I heard the clanking of coins in a payoff. I'd never been to a casino, but I felt my blood pressure and temperature rise along with my excitement.

By the time we got our luggage off the belt, I could see my parents didn't have a plan. They'd been so desperate to leave Stockton; they didn't have a clue what they were going to do next. We ended up downtown in a dirty little motel a few blocks from the Union Plaza Hotel. They paid for a week up front and the moment we checked in and unpacked, Pops took off and didn't return for three days. When he did, I learned he'd lost every penny they'd stolen in Stockton. We were now flat broke. When our week was up, we headed to a homeless shelter. For the next few months, we hit every homeless shelter throughout the downtown area.

The shelters were set up on a first come, first serve basis for each night. Each day we had to get up, leave, and then come back at the specified time that evening to stand in line, hoping that we could get a bed for the night. Most of the shelters kept women and children separated from the men, so we'd be in different quarters than my father. This hard routine became our life.

I enrolled as an eighth grader at Las Vegas High School, which was luckily located right next to downtown, so I could walk to school from whatever shelter we stayed in the night before. Mom would haul my luggage around while I was at school then I'd hook back up with them when I got out. It's hard to admit this but I actually got used to the routine of the homeless. There were a few times here and there when we had money to get a motel room, but most of the time we were bouncing around from shelter to shelter. One shelter we spent time at was like a big house with actual bedrooms, each with two beds. There was even a TV room or common area for everyone. This shelter was only for women and children, so Pops had to stay at the men's house across the street. It was actually nice, but I think the rules were too strict for my parents to handle seeing how we never went back after the one night. The rest were all the same—buildings with small rooms, bunk beds, thin prison mattresses, and a community shower and bathroom at the end of the hall. It was mandatory to attend the nightly Bible study or church service at each shelter in order to get a bed that night.

We stayed at one particular shelter that was just horrible. It was a rundown warehouse filled with the stench of old booze and rotting urine. Everyone slept on a wide-open floor and there were no showers, which forced us to wash up in the sink. The place was overcrowded so we only had a couple of inches to ourselves. There were no mattresses and all we had to sleep on was a spot on the hard floor the size of a blanket for all three of us. The people who filled blankets on every side of us were just as desperate as we were. One time I stood up and saw an endless sea of blankets and people. It looked like a natural disaster. The first night I tried to relax to go to sleep, but I heard a nasty fart echo off the concrete floor followed by an old drunken bum already snoring up a storm. I laid there wondering if there was more to life than this. Was this as good as it got?

Even though this shelter was by far the worst, one day something interesting happened. An old guy who called himself John 3:16, in an even older red painted mail truck rolled in. On the side of his truck were large signs that read, 'Soup, Soap and Hope.' He passed out sandwiches, coffee, donuts, socks, blankets, and other things like that to us homeless people. He was a radical guy who even carried a flask of spiked punch to share with alcoholics who may have had the shakes. He was of course my Pops' favorite. He walked around saying how God loved us and preached some messages, but only after we ate. Seeing someone do that, gave me hope that there was some basic good in all of humanity.

When you're homeless, one of your top priorities is food. The shelters didn't provide any, and unless we received something from John 3:16, we would likely go hungry for the day. This is where the soup kitchens came in. It didn't take long for us to learn the serving times for breakfast, lunch, and dinner at each of the soup kitchens, and each serving time would find us promptly standing in line waiting for our meal. Breakfast was always the same—a bowl of thick, sticky oatmeal, a slice of bread, a boiled egg or artificial scrambled eggs made from a powdered mix, and powdered milk. Lunch and dinner were always the same meal as well—a type of stew with potato chunks and a few vegetables in it, a hard, bread roll that I'd break up and put in the stew, and a glass of powdered milk. This was real life—down and dirty—as low as it could go without being in jail. We were just like the homeless people you see on the streets, except we had just come off a shopping spree and all our clothes were brand new. Other than that, we ate like the homeless, slept like the homeless, and lived like the homeless each day.

This nightmare finally ended one day when we were standing on the street and Mom and Pops got into an intense argument. I'd just about had it with Pops, too. They were going at each other when he took a step towards her as if he were going to hit her. That's when I stepped in front of her, faced him with my fists up, and stopped him in his tracks. We stared at each other for a few seconds and although I was scared to death of what might happen next, I wasn't going to back down. The anger in his eyes burned red as he spat out, "No son of mine would ever stand up against me!" Then he turned and walked away.

Mom got on the phone and called her sister in Seattle and she sent us a couple of plane tickets to get us the hell out of there. A day later, we left Pops in Vegas and flew to Seattle to live with my aunt. For me, this was move number seven.

## *Chapter Six*

We moved into the Springwood Projects in Kent, Washington where my Auntie Kay was living at the time. The only good thing I can say about this place is that it wasn't a homeless shelter. Still, I was grateful to my aunt for taking us in and getting me off the concrete Vegas floor.

The experience in Vegas had taken a lot out of me. On top of that, my father rejecting and disowning me had begun forming an acid inside of me, one that ate away at my heart every day. I needed something to take away the pain. That's when I discovered weed.

The first time I smoked it, someone passed the pipe to me and instead of admitting that I'd never done it before, I just snatched it up and took a puff. Of course, much choking and gasping followed. I truly thought I was about to cough up a lung. Then I grew lightheaded and a little goofy until finally reaching my stride and mellowing out. Within in a few minutes, I was serenely sitting back with my eyes barely open, thinking deeply about every little thing. The acid in my heart was no longer burning. I was hooked.

I started out using a pipe about three to four inches long that had a small metal bowl at the end. Later my pipes were made of ceramic or marble, as only the truly refined chronic smokers used. Chillin' at one of the dope houses drinking forty-ounces of Old English 800 and getting high became the order of the day. Suddenly, life was beginning to make sense. Maybe Pops was on to something.

Of course, I was only thirteen years old and needed to gravitate towards something solid, desperately. I really needed a father figure to take me by the collar and show me how to be a man. And how to respect a woman. And how to live a clean, successful life. But I didn't have that. My options were limited to bad and worse. Most of the guys in this new hood were older than I was and they were all thugs and crack dealers. It seemed that everyone running around my little world was either a dope dealer, a thug, or a crackhead—*clucks*—as we called them. And there was no way in hell I was going to be a cluck. That left me with only one option—to kick it with the dealers.

During the day, I attended the eighth grade at Sequoia Jr. High and maintained decent grades. At night, I learned the dope game. A mere ten days after arriving in Kent, I was already watching guys mixing cocaine with baking soda and cooking it into crack rocks. In the hood, these rocks were diamonds. While DeBeers was busy mining real diamonds from the ground, the homies worked hard at making 'hood diamonds' which looked perfect on a customer's finger, especially when surrounded by a crack pipe. At first I just watched, learned and soaked up everything I could. I learned all the right business methods, from what size to cut the rocks and what quantity to sell for what price, to the proper lingo to use when conducting business. This seemed to be a good gig—a gang of homies hangin' on the streets while the clientele came directly to them. It was like a crack drive-thru. There was plenty of money to go around, so everyone was getting paid big time! But even with knowing all of this, I hadn't yet gotten into the game. I was dead broke. Until one day, something happened that would push me in.

One night a few homies and I walked over to Hoagies Corner to get some food for our munchies. As we were standing there looking at the menu board, I realized I didn't have a dime to my name. I just stood back while everybody else ordered food. The big homie Rayshaun asked me, "Why ain't you getting nothing?" I said, "Cuz I ain't got no money."

He said, "Now listen, I can pay for your food, but I'm not going to because you been with us out here for all this time just watchin' us hustle while you could be getting yo own money the same way we getting ours!" From that moment on, I decided I would no longer be a bystander—I was going to get my share. This is something that I carry with me to this very day: I won't stand by and just observe life. I have to be a part of it. I won't stand by and just admire successful people. I can learn anything that someone teaches me and achieve anything to which I apply myself. If there's no one to teach me, I'll learn on my own and do the necessary steps to achieve whatever I desire. It's just sad this lesson had to come from a drug dealing thug and not a dad. Such is life in the urban jungle called the hood where you take what you can get.

Now that I was ready to become a professional drug dealer, I needed to find a good supplier. I took stock of my surroundings and spotted just the guy—an O.G. named 'Big C'. This guy was moving so much weight in cocaine that he was able to serve up double to us for any amount, small or large. If we came in with $20, he'd give us $40 worth of cooked up rocks. This hook up was only for his crew and he considered me a young block runner. That was all great, but now I had another problem: no money. Since I had no job and definitely no cash, I needed to come up with a plan to get some. I named that plan Operation Cindy.

Cindy was a cute little blonde I talked to frequently at school. I knew she had a crush on me and would likely be an easy mark. I told her I'd gotten into trouble with some guys from the neighborhood and they'd hurt me bad if I didn't come up with the $75 I owed them quickly. Of course, she didn't want me to get hurt and she offered me the money straight away. Funny thing, her mom was a police officer. Fortunately, her daughter had excellent taste in men. Of course, I snapped up her offer and went straight to the big homie to get double up on $75. He shot me $150 worth of rocks and I was in business. I immediately hit the corner with the rest of the crew, but found little success. There were too many of us out there and the clucks were not used to coming to me. As a result, I did terrible that first day. Late that night when everyone went inside and I was walking back to my aunt's apartment, a cluck approached and asked me if I had anything. That's when I realized my shift was late night. When the rest of the boys left to go party, I went out to make money.

To keep my mom from knowing what I was doing, I decided to get a job. Besides, I could always use more money. The problem I had was my age: I was now fourteen and too young to get a regular job that didn't involve a sex offender-like man and a white van. To solve the problem, I took a photocopy of my birth certificate, whited out the 1973 and typed 1971 over it, and then made a clean copy. Now I was the legal working age of sixteen.

With the birth certificate, I soon landed my first job at A&W as a cook making the minimum wage of $3.50 an hour. This meant I was keeping up my grades at school during the day, then working part-time as a cook at A&W and finishing up by selling rocks late at night. Man I was busy! One morning, I was so tired that I was in a deep dream where the police were chasing me for selling rocks. It was bad. I knew they were going to catch and probably kill me when my loud alarm clock went off. This caused me to jerk upright hitting my face on the corner of my dresser, which was right next to the bed. Blood gushed everywhere and I should've gotten stitches but instead my mom cleaned it up, put a Band-Aid on it, and sent me to school. The scar in my left eyebrow reminds me every day of that moment but at least it was better than the beating those cops were gonna give me in my dream.

With money coming in from both my legit job and my dope dealing, my pockets were full. Sadly, I wasn't into investing or storing it like some guys did. A few dealers had stacks and stacks of cash stuffed in shoeboxes in their closets while I blew it all on shoes and clothes. Still, I loved the feeling of having so much cash in my pocket all the time.

\*\*\*

Something began happening in Kent that I wasn't used to: white folks calling me "Nigger." I'd be walking alone or with a homie and a car would drive by with someone yelling out "Nigger!" Whenever this happened, we'd yell back, challenging them to stop the car and face us, but it never happened. One time, I was with one of my homies and we were walking against the flow of traffic along the sidewalk. This car was speeding by with a guy's body hanging out of the window. As they passed us he launched a large McDonald's cup full of ice and soda at us, all while yelling "Nigger!" The cup hit me hard in the gut, causing me to buckle over and fall to the ground. While I gasped for air, my homeboy noticed the car stopped at a red light up the block and took off running. Then the light changed and they took off before he got close enough. I had a bruised stomach for almost a full week after that. I know full well what I went through was nothing in comparison to the struggles and suffering that blacks have endured, but I'll never forget those acts of hatred, ignorance and wickedness for as long as I live.

\*\*\*

I had been dealing rocks for a few months when I met Ricky Simms and Ronny Branford, two brothers who had recently moved to Kent from Portland, Oregon. Ronny and Ricky had different fathers, but shared the same mother. The moment we met, we became thick as thieves—*literally*. I was one of their brothers, so much so that we started telling everyone that we were all brothers. (Over the next few years, these guys would become my best friends) I was hanging out less with the dealers in Springwood and more with Ronny and Ricky, because the things we did were a little more appealing to me.

We spent our time dealing rocks, chasing girls, and rapping. We started a rap group, recorded a few songs, and performed at a few talent shows. Ronny and Ricky had a Mexican homie named Bobby, who lived in the same complex they lived in. Bobby was cool and laid back. He hooked us up with a friend of his who had a studio where we could record our music. As a result, we started hangin' with Bobby too.

One weekend, Bobby's cousin, Hector, came to visit from L.A. We were all just kickin' back on a Friday night with nothing to do when Hector said, "So how would you guys like to go joyriding?"

We said, "What the hell is joyriding?"

He said, "You never heard of joyriding? We can sit here and waste our weekend doing nothing or we can steal a car, drive around the city, and have some fun! That's joyriding."

"You know how to steal a car?" Ronny said.

Hector laughed. "I do it all the time. I could show you just like that!" He snapped his fingers.

We looked at each other and said, "Why not?"

We hung out until midnight, and then walked a couple miles down the road until we got to a different neighborhood. We were on the prowl for any Buick Regal, Oldsmobile Cutlass, or Chrysler LeBaron. The first Regal Bobby found just so happened to be unlocked, so we all jumped inside and watched Hector operate. He took a flathead screwdriver and rammed it into a joint in the steering column, breaking the whole thing off and exposing the piece behind the ignition. This metal piece rotates when the proper key is stuck into the ignition and turned. Hector bypassed the place where the key went and stuck the screwdriver into the rear piece pulling it back towards him. Instantly the car started right up. The whole process had taken less than a minute, which concluded our entire lesson in Car Theft 101. Now, we were professional car thieves just like Hector and a new hobby was born.

High from the adrenaline rush of stealing our first car, we took to the streets and rolled up and down Pacific Highway for two hours looking for something else to get into. Finding nothing, we dumped the car behind a 7-Eleven two miles away from Ronny and Ricky's apartment and walked back. After that night we never saw Hector again, but what he showed us brought many exciting joyrides for months to come.

After a few more joyrides, we decided to get smart and put a system together to avoid capture. Our plan was to drive to a faraway neighborhood, steal a car, and bring it back to our hood to ride around for a couple days. Then we'd dump it and get another one. This worked for months, primarily because we never kept a car longer than three days. One night we were bold enough to go right into a used car lot in the middle of the night and ride off in a Chrysler LeBaron. We weren't even taking these cars to a local chop shop to turn a quick profit. We were simply taking them for our own use.

It didn't take long before we started stealing the contents from the vehicles. Everything from the personal belongings left in the cars to ripping out the tape decks was fair game. We stashed all this stuff in the trunks of the cars that we took which was probably quite stupid.

Two days before Christmas, Ricky, Ronny, and I were riding around in the middle of the night. Ricky decided he wanted to visit one of his girlfriends. We rolled up to the apartment where she lived and parked the car. Ricky went inside to see if she needed anything from him, leaving Ronny and me in the car. While we waited, we decided to blast some music from the speakers. Since it was in the middle of the night and people were sleeping, I'm guessing they weren't too happy about it, because in no time, a high beam light turned the darkness inside our car to noon on the sun. I couldn't see anything.

Shielding his eyes, Ronny turned to me and said, "What happens if we ain't got driver's licenses?"

I said, "What?! Driver's licenses? What about the stolen car and the stuff in the trunk?"

The whites in Ronny's eyes told the whole story. "Oh shit!" was all he could manage.

Of course, the police arrested Ronny and me and took us to the King County Juvenile Correctional Facility. The next day Mom picked me up and asked me what happened. I told her that I had no idea the car was stolen. Sadly, this book will be the first time she'll get the truth about this story. Sorry Mom, I hope you forgive me. Unbelievably, for whatever reason, the owner didn't press charges, the police dropped the case, and our records remained clean.

***

As we continued rapping and doing small shows here and there, we ran into a group called Tramp Alley. Tramp Alley was a band of longhaired, punk rock white boys who began hanging out with us, smoking weed and discussing the world's problems—or mainly smoking weed. Before long, they made us part of their act. At every show they performed, we'd show up during the middle of it, run up on stage like gangsters, and snatch their microphones from them. They'd act as if they didn't know what was happening and we'd burst into a rap song. Everybody in the crowd loved it. We did this all summer long once school let out. After each show, we would party like rock stars. They were much older but they let us drink, smoke and do all sorts of crazy stuff with them.

Sometimes, when we were all high, we'd get some roman candles and use them as weapons on each other. Ronny, Ricky and me would stand apart and light our candles. Then we'd fire them at each other. The fireballs raced over our heads and sometimes stuck into our clothing. Amazingly, we were never injured but we did burn up many clothes. While this was going on, Tramp Alley would watch and sometimes bet on the winner. For some strange reason they didn't want to participate.

Eventually, The Summer of Tramp Alley (as I called it) ended when school was starting up. I was now attending Kent Meridian High School and in the tenth grade. Once school had started, I greatly reduced my drug dealing, especially since I'd added football to my schedule. I was not yet on the varsity squad and though undersized, loved the hitting. Each Friday we had a game and afterwards, I'd go party with my homies somewhere.

One Friday, we were all hanging out at the McDonalds across the street from the school. Ronny and Ricky were there along with a couple of new guys in the crew, Mark and Derrick. There was also a big crowd of kids from our high school. Ronny elbowed me and pointed to Shelly, a new girl who'd just moved here from Texas. He'd been having sex with her, showing her the ropes and all, and now she was standing outside with her sister Tamra.

"C'mon ya'll," Ronny said. "Let's go outside. I want to talk to Shelly."

We agreed and went outside to greet her, but the moment Shelly saw me, she gave me the evil eye. It caught me off guard and I wondered what I'd done to piss her off. From that moment on we hated each other. I told the guys to keep moving and let Ronny have some space with this chick, so we walked to the parking lot and waited for the outcome.

A lot of kids were hanging out there with us and I overheard one girl tell another girl, "That Shelly's a ho!"

"I know," the other one said. "She's sleeping with all the boys in the hood."

It wasn't the first time I'd heard that. Despite her recent arrival, she'd already ridden in many car seats. According to these girls, she was making her way around the boys in the hood, looking for just the right ornament. I figured she'd mess with Ronny for a while, however briefly, and move on to the next homie. A few nights later, we were at the Springwood Projects kickin' back at one of the dope spots, when in she comes with Charles Wright, one of my other homeboys. We all ended up hanging out and getting drunk that night on Mad Dog 20/20 Orange Jubilee. For some reason she hadn't yet given me the evil eye. Later in the evening, I found myself actually having a pleasant conversation with her. I began to think maybe we'd just gotten off on the wrong foot—perhaps she was even cool. Unfortunately, this was the first night I sampled Mad Dog 20/20 and it would be my last. I drank so much I blacked out and woke up in my auntie's apartment lying face down on her floor in a puddle of my own vomit. At least it smelled like orange jubilee. Later, after talking to some of my homies, I found out I was so drunk I couldn't walk home and it was Shelly along with one of my other homies who'd carried me back to my aunt's apartment. When I saw

Shelly at school, she came up and asked how I was doing. That's when she told me about that night and how she was the one who cared for me and made sure I ended up in a safe place. I thought how incredibly wrong I'd been about her. She was actually a nice, thoughtful, caring girl, someone Pops could be proud to have as a daughter-in-law (assuming he ever came back). I started wondering if there could be something more between us. Sure enough, we exchanged phone numbers and in no time, I learned the rumors were true. She was unbelievably seductive, and when she had her homeboy worked into a raging lather, she was quick to drop her panties and give it up. By this time I'd just turned fifteen and had been around the block a few times sexually, but with my out of control hormones, I was always looking for more. Even with everything I'd already experienced, Shelly was something else. When she grabbed a hold of me, I'd fall into a drunken sexual stupor. The things she did to me were not of this world. For a boy with nothing else but sex on his mind literally every minute of every hour of every day, she was just what the doctor ordered. Most days we'd just skip school and do it at her place repeatedly while her parents were at work. Each orgasm was completely different. I couldn't imagine how any human being knew how to do those kinds of things, but soon I stopped thinking about all that and like the Jamaican ATM, I just accepted it as a gift. At this point I became her addicted prisoner—a sex cluck. And she let me feed my unending desire anytime.

Over the weeks of continual supernova sex, I received a nice surprise—I actually began to like her. She was fun to talk to and cheerful. She was actually very engaging, not harsh like some of the hood girls who'd already been beaten and abused. Shelly was interested in what I had to say and what I was doing— almost fascinated with me. It was as if someone had designed the perfect girl for a teenage boy like me— mind blowing sex with all the respect I deserved. It didn't take long before my casual interest turned into something much deeper.

There were times I'd be hanging with the homies and they'd be telling stories of how they'd been with her, some even two at the same time. My heart began to ache as they told these stories and I wanted them to stop, but couldn't let them know I was falling for her. For me it was now more than mere sex; Shelly and I had a genuine connection. We'd be talking about current events and she'd marvel at how much I knew. She would tell me how good-looking I was, how strong my muscles were, and how she was positive I was going to be something big one day. She could just see it. Then, as if she was reading my mind, she'd slide her long, thin fingers like a snake up my leg and into my shorts where she knew I had something important waiting for her. Instantly the conversation would stop and she would make me feel even better about myself. Truly, no drug on earth that affected me the way she did.

Of course, I wasn't the only one who had discovered this gold mine. On more than one occasion, while we were together there would be different guys knocking on her door. These were all guys I knew and ran with in the hood. We never answered the door, but we could see through the peephole who it was. They all went away empty handed. I began to feel like she'd chosen me alone out of all the boys in the hood. I was the special one. I was the one who'd be living with this sexy goddess the rest of my life.

During one passionate moment when my mind and body exploded, I pulled her up close and whispered, "There, I just got you pregnant. Now you'll only be with me." It was a joke, something I didn't really mean, but that's how deep I was into this girl.

We kept up for weeks on end until one day, she said, "Well you got your wish."

"What wish is that?"

"You know the wish you had. The one where I'm pregnant."

"What?! Pregnant?" I said dazed and confused. "But I'm only fifteen. I can't have a baby."

The sexy goddess was gone. In its place was something else, something sinister and mean. She put a hand on hip, cocked her head sideways, and smirked, "What did you think, dickhead? All this was free? No, it's time to pay the price."

I felt a wave a panic race through my body, but calmed myself by thinking of the entire cast of guys who could be the father. I mean, *what are the odds it's mine, huh?*

### *Chapter Seven*

It didn't take long to realize that Shelly wasn't lying. Some poor fool had actually knocked her up. Somehow, she was positive that I was the father and she stuck to that story. But I couldn't help myself from going through a list of all the guys she'd been with (not to mention the ones that I didn't know of). The more I thought of it, the more my initial fear of being the father faded. I was certain it was someone else and she was just trying to rope the guy she thought was the most responsible. Of course, I had to deal with all my homies giving me a hard time, but they also knew the odds were definitely in my favor.

Towards the end of her pregnancy, things got bad between us. So bad, in fact, that I decided to leave town. Ronny and Ricky had moved back to Portland a couple of months earlier and it was a no-brainer to leave home and live with them. Though this was move number eight, it was on me, no one else.

By now, I had reentered the thug lifestyle and had some cash from selling rocks. I was still fifteen, but very street smart. About a week into my stay, Ronny, Ricky, and I were hangin' on the block with a gang of other homies from the neighborhood. It was a little after midnight and we had all been drinking forty-ouncers of Old English 800. For some reason I got into a trash talking battle with this guy named K Dogg. We were going back and forth about who's better than who and who can beat who, foolish crap like that when Ricky jumped up and said, "Ya'll niggas are arguing like bitches! Just settle it now. Fight and get it over with!"

K Dogg said, "Man, Rose don't wanna fight me. He don't want none of this!"

I jerked my head around, stared at K Dogg, and said, "Man you crazy. Ain't nobody scared of you, nigga!"

Just like that, it was on. We jumped into the middle of the street and fought like dogs for at least twenty minutes. We were going hard, exchanging blow for blow and rolling around on the ground. Then we'd stop, get to our feet for a moment or so, and then go back to exchanging blows. This continued until we were both worn out and exhausted. K Dogg hunched over in front of me with his hands on his knees gasping for air. His clothes were torn and bloody as mine were. I was so tired I was about to pass out.

K Dogg finally caught enough air to speak and said, "You done, nigga?"

All I could manage was, "Yeah."

Just like that, it was over. Nobody won that fight, but it was good entertainment for all the boys on the block. One nice benefit was the new respect K Dogg and the rest of the homies had for me in my new home.

***

I'd been slangin' rocks in Portland for two weeks when Auntie Rachel (who lived back in Seattle) called and asked me to help her drive to Stockton. I was always down to help family, so there wasn't any decision to make. She started the drive from Seattle and stopped in Portland to pick me up and south we went.

When I arrived in Stockton, I decided to stay with my other aunt, Auntie Pam, and try to get myself on the right path. I stopped selling crack. I wasn't even smoking any weed. Then I enrolled at Edison High School where I actually went to class—most of the time. For spending money, I got a job at Kentucky Fried Chicken using my fake birth certificate. My previous experience at A&W was impressive to them so they decided to start me out at minimum wage. Now I was selling chicken to people instead of rocks to clucks and making in a week what I could've been making in thirty minutes.

Several months had passed when Auntie Pam began planning a big get-together for Thanksgiving. My job was to bring some chicken from KFC. (Of course, I got a discount on food there.) She was getting a big turkey and fixing up the apartment real nice. Everyone was bringing something. It was Tuesday, two days before Thanksgiving, when Auntie Pam's phone rang.

"Rose, it's for you. It's your mom."

I picked up the phone and said, "Hey Mom, what's up?"

"I'm at the hospital and I got some news for you, son. This is your child!"

"What?! Did Shelly give birth?"

"Yes. Yesterday."

"Uh, how could you know it's mine? Just by looking at her?"

"Trust me, I know. She looks just like you, and I know I'm right about this!"

A week later, I was on a Greyhound Bus headed back to Seattle to meet my daughter.

***

The moment I laid eyes on Desiree something in my soul shifted. I still wasn't convinced I was her father, but I was absolutely in love with this baby. I immediately thought that I'd run out, get a job, and be the best father in the world to this kid. I proposed that we settle down together and be a family. I didn't care about the other guys or anything from her past. We had a baby. A little life that was depending on us to care for her and she was the only thing that mattered. Shelly agreed. I moved into the apartment with Shelly and her sister Tamra, and just like that, we were a family.

I found a job selling subscriptions for the *Seattle Post Intelligencer*. It wasn't much, but it was a start. Both Tamra and Shelly weren't working and Shelly received a welfare check. That made me the only one working. I didn't care how much money I needed to earn or how high the mountain I had to climb. I was going to climb it.

I soon discovered living together with our little daughter was an incredible feeling. Our lives were simply wonderful—for about six days. When the euphoria wore off, I could see all of the same homies, thugs, and relatives as before surrounded us. Every day all the same crap was constantly in my face. And each day was a new fight. It didn't take long to see we were like oil and water; there was just no mixing us. With the same guys still coming around wanting her to drop her panties, it became too much for me to take. After just two short months, I decided to leave and took off to Portland again.

On the streets of N.E. Portland, I jumped back into the dope game by curb servin' rocks to the neighborhood fiends. We called it 'curb servin' because we would stand on the street corner, run up to the cars of clients, and serve them as they passed through. We did it with one quick handshake motion. When you're addicted to crack, you don't want to waste time stopping your car, opening up the door, and getting out. You were losing valuable time when you could be high. I also got a job at Burger King because I always thought it was good to have a job to explain where my money was coming from. Since I was a child, no matter where I was I'd always had a real job.

The last time I'd been in Portland, I'd met a cute girl named Neicy. Now that I was back, I reconnected with her. We began hooking up regularly, mostly late at night in the abandoned house next to where we were staying. We would get drunk, smoke weed and have sex. I started catching feelings for her and began thinking this could develop into a serious relationship. However, after a month, her family up and moved to Connecticut and that was that.

It didn't take long before I missed my daughter, too. So, I packed up and headed back to Seattle. This time I wasn't trying to get back together with Shelly. I only wanted to see my daughter. I had some things at her place, but I wasn't trying to live there. I'd just come and go and see little Desiree. In fact, I was bouncing around from place to place and hangin' with a new crew. These guys weren't the hustling, moneymaking types, but more like straight up thugs. Three of them were my regulars—Kenny, Pig and Tommy. We did crazy things together. One night we hooked up with some white dudes Pig knew and they told us how doing acid would make us hallucinate. "It's gonna be a great ride! You can't go through life and miss this! Really." They sold us on it, so we gave it a shot.

I took the tiny red paper dot and let it dissolve on my tongue. Nothing happened. After two hours, I felt no different. I turned to Pig and said, "These guys are full of shit."
He whispered, "Or they didn't give us the real stuff."

I got up to go talk to them about this bullshit and that's when it hit me hard. I felt like I'd just warped into another dimension. Everything was liquid and wavy. The walls were rippling like thin paper blowing in the wind. The floor had small waves like when you drop a rock into a smooth pool of water. Before we took the dots, they had said, "Whatever you do, DO NOT look in the mirror!" To me, that meant I had to look in the mirror.

I walked on water (the floor) to get to the bathroom and stood in front of the mirror. For the first few seconds, nothing was different. Then suddenly my face started melting away. I could see it literally oozing down to the sink as if I had no bones. I started yelling, "Oh my God! What's happening?!" I worked frantically with my hands to push my dripping face back into place, but it melted right through my fingers, splattering on my shirt and into the sink. I watched in horror as one of my eyeballs slid right down the drain. It was so real that I was terrified and screaming. When the others heard my screams, they busted into the bathroom and pulled me out.

Pig said, "Man, why the hell would you look in the mirror when they told us absolutely to not do that?" "I didn't think anything would happen," I stupidly replied.

A short time later, we left the apartment. Tommy was driving. As soon as the car began to accelerate, it seemed as if we were travelling at warp speed through hyperspace. Lights were flashing by on either side so quickly that I couldn't identify any vehicle. It was like *Star Wars* when they shifted into hyperspace—long streams of lights everywhere. I was terrified, but also amused, confused, and composed. I had all of these emotions impossibly at the same time. We finally ended up sitting around a campfire we had somehow started somewhere in the woods thirty miles from town. On top of that, we'd been spending the time engaged in some seriously deep conversations about government conspiracies and about how the man just wanted to keep us down. I was thinking of things on such a high level that I had a hard time believing it. I was actually thinking about my future. How it would turn out for me. What would I become? Would I die young or would I grow old? After a couple hours of this, I'd had enough and decided to leave the group. I said, "I'm leaving guys" and started walking back to town.

Kenny yelled back, "Wait! It's too far to walk. You'll never make it!"

I said, "Whatever. I'm out of here." I began my thirty-mile walk back to my apartment.

By now, my senses were heightened to Superman strength. I could hear the wings of birds flapping in high fidelity. I could see clearly in the dark for miles ahead of me. I noticed a faint buzzing sound and focused my eyes straight ahead, only to find a tiny bee. It was about 100 yards away yet I could see it crystal clear with my Superman super-vision. I continued to walk towards it while the bee flew straight at me. The closer we got to each other, the louder the buzzing got. Before long, I could see the bee getting bigger and bigger. This carried on for several minutes until we were face to face. In slow motion, I could see the flapping movement of its tiny wings and hear the loud buzzing sound. We came within an arm's reach as the bee flew to my left and went around me, keeping on his way. I continued to hear the buzzing for several more minutes as the volume decreased. Then it faded out altogether. This happened with many other creatures.

By the time I made it home, it was daylight. It had been twelve hours and I was still tripping on this stuff. I found it impossible to sleep, being so wired. In fact, I stayed awake for over forty-eight hours. When I finally came down, I made up for it by sleeping at least twenty-four more hours. Only then did I regain consciousness, and all from one tiny dot. Wow!

A week later, I was walking with the same bunch of guys in the middle of the night. We were just messing around with no real destination. Pig pointed out a shortcut through a Catholic Church parking lot. Sure, we could've walked around the block; it wasn't as if we had an appointment to be somewhere. Instead, we decided to take the shortcut anyway.
When we walked behind the building, I noticed the back door wasn't completely shut. I said, "Yo, let's see what's inside."

We all ran over to the building and I pulled the door open. Just as I was going in, my three homies stopped. I took a few more steps and looked back. No one was following me. Frustrated, I said, "C'mon ya'll, there has to be all kinds of valuables in here!"

The three looked at each other and shook their heads. Kenny finally said, "Man, you know I'm down for anything, but I ain't robbing no church!"

Pig chimed in. "No way we're stealing from a church. Man, you're crazy if you go through with it."

"Yeah, Rose," Tommy said. "That's pretty fuckin' low."

I vividly remember saying, "Man this ain't my religion anyway. If ya'll wanna be cowards then see ya later. I'm goin in!"

I walked down the hall and heard one of them calling out, "Man, you're going to hell! I hear it's warm down there."

I laughed and went through the church, grabbing as much as I could carry. I picked up a VCR and found a large TV, but I couldn't carry it without help. So I went back to the door to yell for my homies to come and help me, but they were nowhere in sight. As a result, all I could get away with was that damned VCR.

When I saw the guys next, they joked about how I was going straight to hell for that one, as if they weren't going to be standing next to me, like they were somehow saved. Kenny said, "The devil's gonna put all your sins on a videotape and play it on that VCR you stole. You'll have to watch it forever."

Pig laughed. "Yeah, but at least you'll be on TV one day—*Hell TV*!"

Little did I know God has His own way of doing things. Sometimes He uses the low of the low—the criminal in our midst—to carry out His plan. All one has to do is keep looking, keep seeking. At that point in my life, the only thing I sought was gratifying my own flesh. I was the only one I lived for.

***

After a couple of months of couch surfing, I finally hooked up with an old friend from my high school who needed a roommate. I pitched in on the rent and he let me stay with him for a while. Of course, he was a straight up thug too.

One night he gave me his car and told me to stay gone for a while—he had a girl coming over.

"Rose, don't fuck up my ride, got it?"

"No problem, Marv. 'Don't fuck up' is my middle name."

"Yeah, that's what I like to hear. I'd hate to plant roses over my favorite Rose."

I took the keys and immediately rounded up my posse—Kenny, Pig and Tommy. Five hours later, like something straight out of a movie, we had cut a path of destruction a mile wide. A gang of Samoans had totally demolished Marv's car. A seventeen-year-old Mexican boy was dead. I was in a police station being questioned by a detective. The room was just like the one on First 48. While I sat in a tiny chair, the two detectives played good cop/bad cop. The good cop came at me first, soft and gentle, explaining that he understood how things can get out of hand sometimes and that I was not in any trouble. All I have to do is say that Pig did it and I'll be free to go. He said that they already had an eyewitness, now they just need me to cooperate. I told them I didn't know anything. Then the bad cop came in and slammed a high school photo of the slain youth on the table getting right up in my face. At the top of his voice, he yelled, "Why are you protecting this guy?! Someone is dead here! Think about his family!"

While little bits of spit flew from his lips, I thought of how I was in deep shit. It was hard to believe it, but I was about to be just like my Pops—a black man in prison with a baby I couldn't support and protect. The two women I had feelings for were just like Mom. I wondered if either of them would visit me in prison. If so, would they wrap up some weed in a balloon, shove it up their vagina, and smuggle it in for me? Watching the cop's lips move, I began thinking of a strategy. If all of us kept our mouths shut, we might scrape through. If one of us talked, the others were dead. Of course, the first one who talked and cut a great deal might also walk free. It was a real dilemma. However, the code of keeping your mouth shut had been hammered into me hard, so I decided to take a chance and hope the others said nothing too.

When someone knocked on the door, the detective came back in and said they had a lead on another car and were kicking us loose. I called Marv who hopped in his girl's car and came to pick me up. He drove me to a deserted area where he questioned the shit out of me while fingering his .38. I realized he was less interested in his Camaro than he was in the law coming after him. Still, I told him the entire truth and hoped he didn't see a reason to blast me. He didn't. With the detective having already identified me, I guess he figured someone would come looking for him when my decomposed bullet-riddled body showed up somewhere, especially since he was last seen picking me up at the police station. On the way back to our place I thought how he might wait a few days, then deal with me. Or the cops would come back and figure out the other car they were chasing had the wrong guys. Either way, I wasn't planning to be around to see how the story ended. I needed to distance myself from this whole situation, so the next day I checked around and got word that one of the homies from the hood was selling an old 1978 baby blue Cutlass Supreme for only $300. It ran good, but the registration and tags were expired. It needed a lot of work to get it to pass both the state inspection and emissions test, but it was just what I was looking for. I did not intend to get it legally registered. I slapped the cash in his palm and hit the freeway headed south back to Stockton.

I ran out of my favorite radios stations to listen to when I crossed into northern California, so I switched over to AM. That's when I heard some preacher yelling and screaming about forgiveness and salvation. I wanted to change the station, but for some reason I couldn't. He talked about all the sins we've committed throughout our lifetime and how Jesus forgives them all. He said we could each have eternal salvation and live in heaven if we'd just accept Jesus as our personal savior. I had to laugh. There was no way Jesus or anyone with any good sense would forgive me for all the terrible things I'd done. Nobody! Right on cue, he brought up how Jesus forgave the thief next to him on the cross, too. Still, I didn't believe it.

Somewhere north of Sacramento, I pulled into a rest area and turned off the car. I just sat there thinking about the words that preacher had said. *Forgiveness. Salvation.* Then I told myself how I knew all the bad things I'd done were wrong, but I'd still done them anyway. I seemed drawn to a dark whirlpool of evil with no way to free myself. That's when I cried out, "Please save me Jesus. Please help free me from this bondage. I'm a slave to my own desires. I just want a better life than this. Please!"

Would this be the wakeup call I needed? Maybe I could change my life and never go back to the evil. I thought about the moment I laid eyes on my baby girl for the first time. In that moment, I wanted to change, to be a completely different person for the sake of this child. I wanted my kid to grow up knowing who her father was, to be proud to call me her dad. I told myself that I'd never subject her to the things that I'd lived through. She'd never have a sleepless night because I wasn't there. She'd never be tormented by the fear of getting terrible news that I'd been murdered. She'd never have to witness me being arrested and hauled off to prison or have to come visit me behind prison walls. She'd never go hungry, homeless or want for anything. Then I flashed back through my entire life and all the decisions I'd made. All I could account for was one bad episode after another. On top of being plagued with losing circumstances, I was making matters much worse with all my terrible decision-making. I had a deep longing within me to be in love and have a normal family and a normal life. I dreamed of being an upstanding, law-abiding citizen. I really wanted to change and be this better person, but I had no idea how to go about it. And even though there were times that I felt I didn't belong in that bad world and hoped to find the way to escape it, the other crabs kept pulling me back down.

Being all cried out, I wiped my eyes and hit the road again. Once I'd been in Stockton for a few days, I talked to one of my homies in Seattle and he told me Pig had been taken in again and confessed to the whole thing. We were off the hook. They later convicted Pig of manslaughter and locked him up for five years until he turned twenty-one. I never saw Pig or any of them again.

## *Chapter Eight*

I arrived in Stockton with a completely new attitude, determined to make good decisions. After a week of loneliness, I called Shelly to talk about healing our relationship, and getting back together. She was receptive. We talked for hours about everything, including my rest stop incident. I told her all that was on my mind, about how I was changing and how I wanted to be this different person. I detailed how I would be there for her and our daughter. I told her I would provide a stable life for all of us. She encouraged me and didn't sound at all like the person who had argued with me and messed around with the other guys. I could tell she had real feelings for me and wanted to be with me, only me. We kept the dialogue going while I sorted things out in Stockton.

Mom and Pops had recently had another child about a year before Desiree was born, a boy named Jamaine. I was now sixteen so that put a fifteen-year age gap between us. I couldn't understand why Mom wanted to have more children, but she was back with Pops and I had to worry about my own life.

After a month of being in Stockton and talking to Shelly every day, we decided to try again. She was so loving and encouraging on the phone, that I couldn't wait to get there to show her the changed man I now was. At the time, she was living with her sister Tamra. They agreed to let me come and stay with them on the condition that I was actively pursuing a new lifestyle. I agreed to get a job quickly, save up some money, and then Shelly and I would get our own place. We were going to do the family thing and do it right.

I put a For Sale sign on that old Cutlass and took it to the Stockton Flea Market. In a matter of minutes, I found a guy who said that there was more than $300 worth of parts on it so he'd take it as is. I was able to get all my money back without doing a thing to it. To me that was a great sign! I was heading in the right direction. With the money, I bought a one-way bus ticket back to Seattle. In my heart, I was serious about changing. This time I was going to get my life right and things would be different for sure. Knowing I had Shelly waiting for me when I got there made the wait bearable.

Of course, wanting to change and actually changing are two different things. Because this bus stopped at every little town along the way, a twelve-hour trip became a twenty-four-hour expedition. That's why I tucked a few joints into my hat—I needed some 'medicine' to get me through the trip. Funny how life is, because I ended up sitting right next to a guy who had a bottle of peppermint schnapps. He was more than willing to share his bottle and during the stops, I was more than willing to share my weed. As we stood behind some building, we puffed away our cares contemplating all the world's problems and knowing every solution had to include free booze and weed for everyone. That was the most enjoyable bus ride I'd ever taken.

We stopped at one town with a one-hour layover. Across the street, I saw a Fred Meyer store and knew they had a jewelry department. My determination to do right by Shelly and my daughter was so strong; I decided to buy a ring for Shelly, just to show her that I was serious. I found a gorgeous one-carat ring for $2,000. With the weed and the schnapps percolating through my brain, I decided to buy it. When the lady asked if I wanted to pay cash or credit, I dug into my pocket and saw I had only a $100. She snapped the box shut and pulled out a skinny gold ring with a diamond she had to show me through a magnifying glass. I wanted more. What could I do? I was a little low on cash.

With the ring in my pocket, I headed back to the bus excited about my future and knowing I still had one more joint left to burn. After my friend and I drained the last of the schnapps and finished off the weed, we hopped on for the final leg home with an excellent attitude.

When I finally arrived in Seattle, it was a happy reunion. Shelly was there with my daughter and I knew immediately I'd made the right choice. After things had settled down it was time for the present. I closed the door to her bedroom, took her hand, and produced my gift. "Let this ring be a symbol of my commitment to change and go straight. This is my promise to you." She hugged me tightly. "Baby, you are a wonderful man and I'm lucky to have you. Now come and get some of the lovin' I've been saving up just for you. And I hope you have some energy, because I've been very lonely." It didn't take me long to get my energy level up, about a whole second. We had a great night and afterwards, I just lay there staring up at the ceiling thinking how lucky I was not to be in prison or killed. Then I drifted off to a deep, restful sleep.

The next morning, I jumped up out of bed and looked for a job. That afternoon landed one as a dishwasher at the Keg Steakhouse for minimum wage. Sure, I could make more in ten minutes slangin' rocks than I could working all week, but when you change, you leave all that behind. I just knew everything was going to be perfect.

A few days later, I had an itching sensation in my genital area. Because I sweat a lot, I figured that maybe I got a little sweaty and needed to take a shower. That didn't help and it got increasingly worse, eventually turning into an uncontrollable, unbearable itch. That's when I started to worry. I decided to talk to Shelly about it.

I pulled her into the bathroom and lowered my voice. "Hey, I just want to let you know that when I was in Stockton I didn't have sex with anyone and since I've been back, you're the only one I've been with, and there's something I need to tell you. I'm embarrassed and I'm scared, because I don't want to lose you and you're all I got, so we gotta talk about this."

"What is it?" she said.

"Something's wrong down there," I said pointing down to my genital area.

"What exactly do you mean, baby?"

"I'm itching like crazy and it won't stop."

"Let me see."

I pulled down my pants and let her look. That's when she hit me with it. "You got the crabs. I can see them everywhere. It's not your fault. I gave them to you. I had them just about the time you came back."

My blood pressure rose. "What dirty dog were you with that gave you crabs?!"

"I don't think you wanna know, baby."

I felt like a volcano about to blow. "I don't wanna know? I have to know who it is! How can I be different and you're still doing the same old shit? You might as well tell me now since you told me that much."

She paused. "Well...it was *either* Ronny or Ricky."

"Ronny *or* Ricky?! They're brothers. You were with both of them? And so close together that you don't even know which one of them gave you crabs?! And now I've got it? Oh shit, you're fuckin' unbelievable!" Then I walked out of the bathroom and immediately went to a clinic where I was treated.

On the way back, I felt reality punching me square in the face. I felt like a damn fool. Again! I had bent over backwards to prove to her that I would change so that she'd let me back into her world, so we could share our daughter's life together as a family. But the cold reality is that her world was a nasty, filthy, cesspool of wickedness. Underneath those sexy seductive curves dwelt a serpent who desired to rip me apart. I was just passing a liquor store when I decided I was done with her. I had to do this carefully. I didn't want to up and run away from Desiree again, so I'd have to play it cool for a while until I could put together an exit strategy.

With this new development, my desire to change started to fade. Sure, my mind was changing somewhat, but most of my actions remained the same. I needed to act on what I was thinking before it would be too late. Up until now, it was all about having a crew and being down with a gang, but after the Pig incident, I was done with all that. Running with gangstas and thugs always yielded the worst results, so I set out on my own. From now on, I'd roll as a solo act.

I kept a low profile, but one day I bumped into a guy I knew who also knew the girl Neicy that I used to mess around with before she moved to Connecticut. She told this guy and he found me and said she was back in Portland, pregnant and telling everyone that I was the father. At this time, I was sixteen years old with one kid already and supposedly another one on the way with a different girl. I hadn't seen this girl or heard from her personally, so I figured it was all just a rumor and paid no attention to it.

One day, while I was working my shift at The Keg, the office told me I had a call waiting. To my surprise, it was Neicy.

"Roosevelt, I had to track you down. I need to let you know I'm pregnant with your baby. I'm about to have it soon, like any day now."

I was speechless.

"Are you still there?"

I couldn't speak for a while, but finally, I was able to put some words together. "Are you sure that I'm the father?"

"Yes, I'm sure. You're the only one I was with."

"Well...I'm at work and I can't really talk about this right now, so give me your number and I'll call you back when I get off."

She gave me her number and I started calling her daily, away from Shelly. We talked, trying somehow to reacquaint ourselves. It wasn't easy over the phone. In fact, it was much easier having sex and not caring about the consequences than it was trying to have a real relationship. I was quickly discovering that a solid relationship took work. Lots of work.

Eventually she gave birth to a boy—Eurico Drakkar Sargent. Since I wasn't there, I had nothing to do with the name. Later people called him Rico and folks would always think he was Hispanic. All Neicy could say was, "I liked the name" as to why she gave it to him.

I decided to go to Portland a week later and see the boy. I pulled up outside her apartment complex and finished off a bomb chronic joint. Even though my eyes were red and barely open, I felt relaxed and ready for what may come. I got to the door, took a deep breath, and knocked. Neicy threw the door back and, with her arms wide open, gave me a big hug. She was just as cute and petite as I remembered and her body seemed completely unaffected by childbirth. Standing in the front room were three women: her sister Charity, her mother Margaret and her grandmother Mrs. Johnson. Neicy introduced all of us. While I was smiling, trying to smooth some Roosevelt charm over the ladies, Mrs. Johnson approached me and stared hard into my eyes, my barely open red eyes.

"Son, I want you to read this." She handed me a Bible that was open to a passage. "Start here and read it aloud."

I thought about saying no, but it wasn't worth ruining the moment. I was flying high, so there wasn't much she could do to bring me down. I lifted the Bible up to my eyes and tried to focus. Then I read:

"Or do you not know that your body is a temple of the Holy Spirit within you, whom you have from God? You are not your own, for you were bought with a price. So glorify God in your body."

Instantly I was no longer high. I was clearheaded and sober. I felt warmth in my heart that I had never experienced before, and it was in that moment that I realized the Bible was not just another book. I knew without a doubt that God just touched me. That preacher on the radio was right after all.

As I blinked my eyes, taking in a whole new world, Neicy said, "Are you ready to meet your son?"
"Absolutely!" I replied.
She led me over to the bassinet, picked him up, and handed him to me. "Meet your son, Eurico Drakkar Sargent. Here he is."
Then it happened again. All the thoughts and emotions I had when Desiree was born came bubbling up. I studied the boy for any resemblance and right off, I could tell he had the lower part of my face.
"Hey, he has my chin!"
Neicy smiled. "He sure does. Isn't he wonderful?"

At that moment, I didn't want to leave him. My desire for being in love and having a family was back, strong as ever, with the hope that this could finally be it. Now I'd been touched by God. The permanent change I so badly wanted was within my grasp. All I had to do was reach out and take it, but could I do it?

## *Chapter Nine*

After leaving my son, I drove back to Seattle feeling like a different person. All the talk of me trying to become a different person seemed so far away, because now I actually felt like a different person. My heart was different. As I pulled up to my apartment, I didn't want to be in Seattle anymore. I knew there was no way that I'd ever be able to coexist with Shelly, and I knew that nothing could stop me from being Desiree's father. I longed for a true family life, something I'd dreamt about for many years. I was curious about the feeling that I'd received from reading the Bible. I kept telling myself that Portland was only a couple hours away from Seattle. I could drive back and forth as much as I wanted to see my daughter. Somehow, I was convinced my life would be better in Portland.

Of course, the first thing Shelly and I did was start fighting again. Every freakin' day. Also, there was always drama from outsiders who surrounded Shelly like a plague. It didn't take me long to pack up my stuff, say goodbye to Shelly, and hit the road.

When I landed back in Portland, I moved in with Neicy and her mother Margaret, who was a real ballbuster. Every day she pounded the Bible and the church into me. She did not let up. If Margaret got tired, she tagged her mother Mrs. Johnson, who climbed into the ring and hammered on me for a while. I know I needed it, but man it was tough to take. Since I was on the straight and narrow plan, I needed to find a good job. It only took a day to find one. Rundell Products was the name of the company. It paid better than minimum wage and that made a big difference. This gave Neicy the ability to stay home and take care of our son. Of course, she was only fifteen so getting a job would've been difficult.

I worked all week and an occasional Saturday. On Sunday, I was right there in church, sandwiched in between Margaret and Neicy. As the preacher went on, I found myself on the edge of my seat, leaning forward, absorbing every word he spoke. Total forgiveness and eternal salvation was still a hard concept for me to get my hands around, yet I felt different seeking Christianity. It somehow felt real. Before, when I got drunk or high, I had to have a substance in me to bring out the effect. But, this Bible and Jesus stuff was something I could feel with absolutely no substance in me. It was truly the power of God.

However, it's hard to stop a freight train, especially one hitched to a hundred cars of misery and bad decisions. Even while I made progress, I continued to dabble in the dark side. Not only did I know it was wrong, but I was sure Margaret and Mrs. Johnson knew I was doing it. That's why they continued to hit me over and over again with Bible passages. They were determined to stop that train cold.

I couldn't wait to ditch Margaret's apartment and get our own. Finally, after several months of saving up my money, I was able to swing it. We moved what little stuff we had over to the new place and I was finally able to breathe. For sure, I was changing, but now I didn't have her family breathing fire and brimstone down me every second. I could relax a little.

My hard work at Rundell Products soon earned me a raise. With more money, we could afford a few more things. I thought life was getting better but we constantly argued. We were just kids and had no idea how to be respectful to each other, let alone to parent. When I got mad, I usually left the apartment and roamed the streets carrying my anger with me. That's never a good recipe for a righteous life.

Six months into my new life in Portland, I got a call from my brother that Mom and Pops weren't doing well. Pops was running the streets again and Mom was addicted to crack. I pounded the counter hard. I knew there wasn't anything I could do for them. I was barely supporting my own family, or at least one of my families. I talked to Mom on the phone and confirmed she was smoking crack. I continued calling regularly until after a month of this craziness, my older brother Lavon stepped in and took my baby brother from her before the state of Washington came and took him away to foster care. This got Mom's attention so she checked herself in to a drug rehab to try to get sober. It was a good first step. As for Pops, he wasn't going to change. He was too far-gone. There would be no rehab for him.

After Mom had been in rehab for several weeks, I drove back up to Seattle to visit her. We mostly talked about my two children, but we also talked about her and Pops. She was beginning to understand that she was addicted to my father: no matter what happened, she just couldn't get free of him. When he went off the rails, it took her down with him. When I thought about it, I realized this mirrored my relationship with Shelly. She was doing the same thing to me. I was somehow able to break free of her, while Mom and Pops were still connected.

Back in Portland, I carried Mom's misery around with me for a while, adding another car to the long line I was already pulling. For the few glorious moments in church when I felt all my pain and suffering lift, it was freeing. When I got out of church and back into my everyday life, it was heavy again.

Mom eventually got out of rehab and went back to her apartment and back together with my baby brother. I could tell she was still lonely, so I began talking to Neicy about moving back to Seattle to live with her. She liked the idea, so we began organizing things to make the move. That's when we ran in to a roadblock. It was Margaret. There was no way she was letting Rico leave Portland. Not with two children who could barely support themselves. After thinking about it, we decided to let her take care of Rico while we went to Seattle. It was like having a permanent babysitter.

I found another job as soon as I hit Seattle. I was now a door-to-door salesman carrying around this huge bag of products. I sold things like coloring tablecloths for kids and cheap trinkets. I was a very good salesman and pulled in about $75.00 a day. Since I didn't have a car, I was just walking, catching the bus, and lugging this huge bag around.

During the hours I didn't work, I always took the time to visit with Mom and Neicy. They kept each other company while I was gone and when I was there, it was always time for celebration. That meant it was time to spark one up. Even though Mom was out of rehab, weed was kind of like smoking cigarettes—it wasn't a *real* drug. There was nothing like having some nice family time while passing a joint around. The high seemed to bind us together. Of course, I'd been going to services less and less now that I was away from the church ladies. It's always hard to read anything, much less a Bible, when there's so much smoke and haze in the air.

As time went on we began to miss our son and Neicy missed her family. We talked it over and now that Mom was pretty stable—only smoking weed and drinking alcohol—we decided to head back to Portland. Another factor for me leaving was my relationship with Shelly. I'd been seeing Desiree and figured since our relationship was good, driving up to see her wouldn't be much of a problem. It was only two hours—certainly no big deal to see my oldest child. Back in Portland, I'd be with my son. I would've liked to be with both of my kids in one city but I couldn't. So even though it was like trying to ride two horses that kept moving further apart, in the end, I felt like I couldn't be without my son. Like so many times in my life, it was time to move again.

Leaving Mom behind was much easier than it could have been, because Pops had finally resurfaced and come home. Even though it only meant Mom's apartment would now be his base of operations again, at least Mom was happy to see him. Of course, he *was* my father. It was hard not to root for the guy.

We arrived in Portland and moved in with Margaret. Soon, Neicy and I were fighting again. Rundell Products had hired someone to replace me so I had to get a job with Burger King at minimum wage. I was disappointed with that but at least it was a job. With every day under Margaret's guard tower, I knew I'd have to save up my money so we could get our own place, and that's what I did. But that didn't stop the fighting. We just didn't know how to be adults.

On my goal to change permanently, Margaret and Mrs. Johnson had me back in church and back on the Bible. That was a good thing. With each message that was pounded into me and with every Bible reading, my attitude slowly began to shift again. It wasn't huge but I could feel the freight train making a slight turn to the good.

Then I turned eighteen. On one hand I was excited and on the other somewhat afraid. Right now the scorecard of my life read: two children with two mommas in two different cities. If I wasn't careful, I had a chance to beat my grandfather's record of twenty-six plus kids running around. Even though I was trying to change and be good, I still felt the pull from the dark side. I still had an eye for the ladies. I often snuck off to be with some girl I'd met in the neighborhood. Neicy suspected as much, but she couldn't catch me. One place my girl and me liked to hang out was Jay's Market. The Indian people who ran it were very nice, so nice they sold alcohol to underage kids without ever asking for ID. You can imagine why everyone liked to hang out there.

One evening, I told Neicy I was working late and slipped away to be with my little squeeze. My buddy Carlos—Neicy's cousin—and his girl planned to meet up with us at the kick it spot. We pulled up to Jay's Market, bought some booze, and then relaxed in the cars with our girls. While we were making out, we failed to notice the car rolling up into the space right next to ours. As I was getting it on with my girl, I glanced through the window and saw Neicy staring at me from the car next to me. She pressed her puzzled face against the window making a small fog circle below her lips. In the front seat was Margaret, who also had her face up against the window, frowning. Instantly, I freed myself of the girl and jumped out of the car to explain myself. Actually to concoct some lie that they might fall for. My jaw was moving fast, spewing out some of that Roosevelt bullshit when Neicy grabbed my collar and pulled me close.

"No, no, no," I said. "It's not what you think. It's not what you think." Actually, it was exactly what they thought.

Neicy was a fighter though and she wouldn't let me go. Margaret's husband started moving in closer as if he was going to take a swing at me when a bunch of my gangsta buddies who were also hanging out there began moving in, ready to jump on them. I held my hands up to my buddies and yelled, "No! This is my family. Just back up and calm down. This is my baby momma and her family." They stopped, but didn't back away. These guys loved to fight and they were looking for any excuse to get it in. I was talking calmly to Neicy, but she wouldn't let me go. I tried one last time to reason with her. "Let's just be cool right now. We're in a public place. Let's talk about this later." I looked over for some help from Carlos, but I hadn't been paying close attention because he must've bailed out the other side of the parking lot the minute the car pulled up next to us. After a few minutes of all this, I got tired of her holding on to me so I knocked her hand off my collar. That's when Margaret's husband jumped me along with the rest of her family. Unfortunately, that was just the excuse my homies needed to get involved. In seconds, they had Margaret's husband on the ground beating the crap out of him—literally! They beat him badly. This gave me a chance to defend myself from the women and push them back. With her husband on the ground, Margaret diverted her attention to him allowing me to flee the scene. I roamed the streets waiting for things to calm down and finally made my way back to our apartment. I had my speech all planned out along with a large jar of my special Roosevelt charm whipped up and ready to spread on thick. When I approached the front door, I found a trash bag with all of my clothes in it. I picked up the bag and said, "So this is how it's gonna be huh? Fine. So be it."

I drove over to a buddy's house and asked if I could spend the night. He said sure and showed me to a spare bed. When I undid the garbage bag, I found Niecy had ripped all of my clothes to shreds. Every single one! I didn't have anything but the clothes on my back. But, since I just cashed my check, I did have a pocket full of money. The next day I went shopping and I bought all new clothes. I lived with my buddy until I got my own place a few weeks later.

The one thing about not supporting your child financially is that eventually, the baby's momma will call you up looking for some of that support. When that call finally came, I started working my magic, knowing that she was looking to forgive me anyway. After several weeks of more punishment, we made up. Since she'd given up our apartment, she and Rico moved in with me. The next time I saw Carlos, I told him he owed me big time for taking the fall on all that mess. He apologized, but told me he just had to get out of there. There was no way he was going to let the Bible thumpers hammer him. To make it all up to me, he was going to hook me up with two of his cousins, Mickell and Anthony. Besides being brothers, they were also cousins of Neicy. The reason he thought we might like to hang out with each other (besides smoking weed) was the fact they we all loved music. He took me to their place and sure enough, these guys were good. Mickell was a dope beat maker and Anthony was a great rapper, a guy with a lot of talent. I'd been rapping some too, so what started as battle rapping against each other turned into a party and us just having fun rapping together. I started hanging out all the time with these two guys smoking weed and rapping. It was so cool; I told Carlos we were now even. Now that I was gone all the time doing my own thing, Neicy got mad. That anger turned into even more fights. Sure, we'd eventually make up and have great sex, but we just fought all the time. Somehow, things rocked right along for almost a year until I turned nineteen and she was seventeen. Then she got sick. At first, I wasn't really paying attention, because she was a petite girl anyway. Eventually I could tell she was losing too much weight. She couldn't hold any food down. While I wasn't a doctor, it looked like anorexia to me. I took her to the doctor and waited outside for the news. He ran various tests before he called me into his office for a chat. I knew it was worse than I thought when Neicy wasn't there.

"Where is she?" I asked.

"The nurse is with her. She's sick right now."

I nervously rubbed my hands together. "Okay, so what're we lookin' at Doc?" I gripped the armrests ready for the worst.

"Well, we ran the tests and I believe I can tell you with certainty that she's pregnant. Congratulations."

I blinked several times. "Uhh, pregnant?"

"Yeah, you know like when a baby comes out?"

"No, I get it. It's just that I was expecting something else, like she had some disease. So I guess this is good news then."

"Yes, it is and she'll need to begin prenatal care soon. I understand she's had one child already so she should have a routine pregnancy. However, I have a list of things she can do . . ."

At that point, I tuned him out. I was feeling the walls closing in around me. I was about to have a third child. This couldn't be. I was barely nineteen. I couldn't support what I had, much less another kid. No, this was bad. I did *not* need to have another child. No way! I found Neicy and we said nothing as we walked to the car. On the way home, I finally spoke up. "Hey, we need to really think about this, okay? Let's not tell your mother or anyone else until we sort this out. Got it?"

"Yeah, I got it," she said quietly.

She knew exactly what I meant. When we got back to the apartment—my ghetto apartment—we sat down and looked at each other. We had dropped off Rico with Margaret during the appointment, so we had the place to ourselves. Then, I sparked one up and took a long pull waiting for the weed to take effect. I passed it to her so she could get her mind right. Then, when we were both thinking straight, I started in. "We don't need this baby. I hate to say it, but we don't."

Neicy lowered her head and stayed silent.

"Look, I can't do this one. Things are spinning out of control. I'm trying to change, but these roadblocks keep popping up in front of me. And this is one roadblock we can get rid of."

Again nothing.

"I want you to schedule an abortion and don't tell no one. No one! If your Bible thumping momma and grandmother find out, they gone trip out. They'll literally kidnap us until the baby is born. Understand?"

Still she said nothing as she stared at her stomach and rubbed it.

"I mean, do you agree with me?" I took another long hit. "Am I talking to myself here?"

When she raised her head, I could see the tears forming in her eyes. "Yeah, I understand. I know it's for the best. It's just that it's gonna be hard to kill a baby inside me. Real hard."

"Yeah, I know it. But when you can't feed it and we're on the street, then tell me how it feels. Okay?"

She nodded as I passed her the joint for some more clear thinking. We said nothing more about it that day. The next morning she scheduled 'the procedure' for Friday, just two days away. The clinic required payment in advance so I had to hustle to come up with the dough, but come up with it I did.

On Friday morning, I helped her to my car. "Don't worry. After this is over, we'll rest up, attend church on Sunday, and forget the whole thing. No one ever has to know but us. Okay?"

"Okay."

I let out a deep breath and leaned back in the seat of my most prized possession: my 1980 Malibu Classic. It was perfect. I had it all decked out with chrome wheels and house speakers in the trunk. Believe me, when I turned up the speakers, you could hear me beatin' up and down the entire block. Everyone knew me by this car. It was my trademark, and because of that, I kept it in great condition. Now its job was to carry my girl and me to the clinic, so we could have a tiny 'procedure' and get back to normal. And with the forgiveness stuff that I knew Jesus offered, I could surely add this small thing to that list.

I reached up and turned the key. Nothing. I jiggled the key and turned it again. Again, nothing. Not one sound. I figured I didn't have the key all the way in so I took it out and reinserted it. Then I turned it again. Nothing.
"What the fuck?" I said. This bad boy has never let me down." I tried the ignition one more time and again it didn't start. "Shit, the battery's dead. I'm gonna grab Ray Ray and get a jump. Be right back."

Ray Ray was a hood mechanic that made extra money getting cars running. Or made them legal. Or chopped them up if need be. Ten minutes later Ray Ray had his car next to mine and jumper cables stretched over. He revved up his engine running for about five minutes then yelled out, "Okay Rose, crank it up!"

I turned the key and nothing. Not a freaking sound. Ray Ray turned off his car and spent another twenty minutes looking over the car before giving me the verdict. "Bro, you got more than a dead battery. You got some kind of ignition problem. This thing ain't even sending an electrical signal to the battery. You're gonna need to have it towed to a shop and taken apart. Sorry for the bad news."

"Yeah man, thanks for your help. Really." I palmed a joint in his hand and he unhooked his cables and drove off somewhere. I climbed back into the driver's seat and tried the ignition one more time. Nothing. Neicy hadn't moved through all this. Now, we simply looked at each other. We knew what was on the other's mind, but didn't want to say it. Finally, I had to say something. "You know, it's like we were not supposed to make this appointment."

She nodded. "Yeah, you're right."

I reached over and held her hand. Then we smiled at each other and got out of the car. Because I didn't have enough money to have it towed to a shop and repaired, I just left it right there and never drove it again. Ever!

## *Chapter Ten*

All that day we said nothing about it. We spent the day sitting next to each other watching TV. At five, I had to go to work flipping burgers so I left her on the couch. When I got home, she and Rico were in bed asleep so I took the opportunity to light one up and think about all this. I knew that as soon as we told Margaret and Mrs. Johnson we were pregnant again, they'd be pushing us to get married. Maybe getting married wasn't so bad. Neicy was very attractive and sexy. Of course, she was the mother of what would soon be my two children. She'd always been faithful to me, even while I'd been...uh, less than perfect. She might just be the best one I'll ever find.

Then I considered her family. Of all the families with cute girls, they were probably the best when it came to the Bible, church, and Christianity. I knew for sure I wanted to change. Becoming a permanent part of her family would likely be the only chance for me to get off this highway to hell because I knew for sure these people wouldn't let me fail. If we got married, I was going to give up weed, drugs, and all the foolishness that enslaved the rest of my homies into a life of addiction, violence, incarceration, and death. I'd devote the rest of my life to Christianity. That long freight train I was pulling was coming to its final turn. The more I thought about it, the more it made sense. There wasn't ever going to be a better situation than this. The only negative was we really didn't love each other. There were no butterflies. We based our relationship on the lust of the flesh—our two kids proved that. However, lust can only take you so far. I took a pull on the joint. My desperation to go straight made this an easy decision.

We discussed it the next morning and broke the news to Margaret. As expected, she blew a gasket at the pregnancy, and then just as predicted, celebrated our decision to get married. Mrs. Johnson was more subdued, but generally approved. I could tell she'd seen many things over the course of her life—that's why she didn't get too riled up about this. Even Margaret's husband, who'd recovered from the ass whipping my homies had rained down on him, seemed satisfied that my connection to those thugs would soon be broken. It seemed to be a win-win situation for everyone.

The day we got married, we had to ride with Margaret to the Justice of the Peace. Neicy was only seventeen and her mother had to give permission in writing and sign some documents at the courthouse. We then paid the fee, had a two-minute ceremony and got our marriage license. There was no kiss or anything (though we had done plenty of that to get us to this point); the whole thing was very businesslike. Afterwards we went back to Margaret's apartment for some small desserts, and then went home. I had to work a late shift, so I kissed Neicy goodbye and left. It wasn't much of a wedding day.

A few days later, I called Mom and told her we'd gotten married. She thought that I was much too young and not ready for marriage but I think she was happy for the new life I was trying to pursue. Pops was still hanging out at home, so that was good. Now, it was as if she had a regular family again, all under one roof. It was something she and I had struggled so hard to achieve. Towards the end of our conversation, she cleared her throat and got serious. "I have to tell you things are going bad for your daughter."
I stiffened. "What do you mean *bad*?"

"Shelly lost her place to stay and is on the streets with Desiree. They don't have any money and are looking for something. She asked me for a place to stay, but I said I'd have to talk to you 'cus I don't want to cause any drama. And that was a few days ago. I don't know where they are now, maybe a shelter."

I felt my anger rising then suddenly cool. "Mom, of course you can give them a place to stay! I'm leading a Christian life now. Besides giving up weed and drugs, I'm reading the Bible and going to church. Forgiveness is now a big deal in my world. Anything's better than having my daughter on the streets. I'll tell you what; I'll take a bus soon and bring you what I can afford. Okay?"

"That'd be nice. I'll make some calls and see if I can get them over here." She hesitated and I thought she was about to hang up when she added, "Son, I'm real proud of you. Lord knows you probably never heard that before, but I just wanted to say it once in my life. I'm *real* proud of you."

I swallowed hard. She was right; I'd never heard those words. "Thanks Mom. I'll let you know when I'm coming back. Okay?"

"Okay son. Take care."

I hung up the phone and thought about my daughter being on the streets. If I was making more money, I could send them more and maybe keep this from ever happening again. However, I had one kid here, plus another one coming. The bills were up to my neck and almost over my face. I was a very hard worker, but starting at minimum wage and working upwards was a tough way to go. The pressure of providing a straight and honest life was huge. No wonder so many men simply bounced and never looked back. With no mentoring or role models, we were crawling through the desert blind. At least now I had the Bible as my guide. Deep down I knew that Jesus was all I was going to need.

I soon made friends at church and it unexpectedly paid off. One of my Christian brothers got me a new job at Super Printers working in their bindery department. They were large and had a ton of customers. My job was to cut down the sheets of business cards to individual card size, fold the sheets of paper for other orders, hole-punch when needed, and generally do all the finishing work. I worked hard, which had never been a problem, and they quickly took a liking to me. It was a very short time before they were giving me more money and more responsibility. It seemed like everything was looking up.

Once I had some extra cash, I took a bus to Seattle and walked to my parents' apartment. Mom was there to greet me with a big hug and right behind her was Desiree. They loved on me as if I'd just come back from the war. Once that was out of the way, I walked to the kitchen and saw my father playing solitaire. He didn't look up from the cards.

"Hey Pops, how ya doin'?"

"Okay," he said, not lifting his head to make eye contact.

"Good. That's real good." It was strange that he wasn't even acknowledging me, but I figured he was having trouble adjusting to the new me, the new *Christian* me. It happened to many of my friends who suddenly didn't want to be around someone who was living clean.

I heard the bathroom door open and footsteps coming down the hall. Shelly appeared and joined Pops at the table.

"Hey Shelly, you doing okay?"

"Yeah, I guess."

"Good. I got some cash for you. Here, take this and I'm gonna give Mom and Pops some money too, for taking care of you. This money will help you get Desiree some clothes or whatever you want." I handed her the money.

"Thanks Rose. Thanks a lot." She seemed to mean it genuinely.

The rest of the visit I spent with Desiree and Mom in the living room catching up. Later, when I left, Pops and Shelly stayed at the kitchen table while my Mom and Desiree hugged me to death. I had tears as I walked away towards the bus home. It was sad, but I'd made that life and I'd have to deal with. At least the Holy Spirit filled me now. That would help me find a way to set it all right.

*** 

Our baby girl was born in June and once again, my heart melted. I wanted to give her the best I could and this time I finally had a shot. I'd hustled my way up to bindery supervisor and was now making enough so we could live like normal adults. It was such a great feeling! To honor my mother, we named her Arkita Renee Sargent. With Mom having survived everything she'd been through and our baby having survived us almost aborting her, it was only fitting. When I told Mom, she was very touched that we'd named our daughter after her.

Neicy and I were doing well, though we still argued a lot. She was a good mother and with me working all the time, we didn't see much of each other, so at least the arguments weren't constant. The most time we spent together was when we were at church, which was a lot. Each time I entered the Lord's house I felt relaxed and free of my past. All I had to do was cross the threshold and my urge to smoke weed or do drugs was completely gone. I couldn't even imagine a circumstance where I'd go back to it.

I was now making enough to move to a better apartment complex. It was still the ghetto, but a step up. The next thing I was saving my money for was a new ride. When we moved, my 1980 Malibu Classic was still there in the parking lot gathering dust. I decided now I wanted a family car, something that didn't scream 'gangsta.' That's why I didn't spend the money to fix it and instead waited for someone to steal it.

After a few evenings in our new place, someone knocked on our door. I opened it up to see Carlos, my buddy from the liquor store incident. "Hey Rose, how you been?"

"Great Carlos, how you been?"

"Can't complain. And guess who's with me?"

I looked behind him and it was Mickell, my old rapping beat making homeboy. "Rose, why you been hidin' out on us?"

I smiled and hugged them both. "I'm married and have two children, in case you didn't know."

Carlos laughed. "Yeah we know all about that. You're a regular family man."

We all found chairs. "What are you guys doing in my hood?" I asked.

Carlos lowered his voice. "We got a drug deal to do a few doors down so we thought we'd stop in and say hi before we did it."

Mickell looked at me. "You want to smoke some after we do the deal? We can come back. Besides I'd like to know what you been up to."

I moved closer to Mickell. "Listen here, God got my heart bro, for real. This is what I'm doing." I picked up a Bible.

"What? You goin' all religious?"

"Yeah, and you need to hear some of this."

Surprisingly Mickell didn't move. Instead he stayed there and listened to me go on and on about Jesus and being saved. In fact, he was so intrigued he decided not to go through with the drug deal and sent Carlos on his way without him. An hour later, I led him to the Lord and he accepted Christ as his savior right there in my living room. From that night forward, Mickell and I were tight again.

Over the next several months, Mickell and I got back into making music. I rapped and he laid down the beats. It wasn't long before Anthony showed up and wanted to do some rapping too. Of course, he also wanted to smoke some weed so we had to sit him down and set him straight. He was resistant but over time, he came over to Christ. With all three of us believers, we turned to making Christian rap music, which in 1993, was still a brand new thing.

VICTORIOUS UNDERDOG

We formed a group and called it *S.4.G.* (Serious for God). We only played small clubs and events at first and not really making any money from it. Neicy was supportive, especially since I wasn't living the life I used to lead. Over time, we built up a nice local following, and I have to say we were talented. After a while, we were able to save up enough money to put together a demo tape. I began sending it all over and landed a huge gig at the Portland Expo Center. A big local church called Victory Outreach was holding two drama shows there—one on Saturday and another on Sunday. They were expecting at least 5,000 people. Unbelievably, they let us open up both shows. It was a huge break. When I got the word, I called the guys together and told them we needed to have some product to sell. They agreed but we were short on dough. I had already called Discmakers, a well-known production house and they told me we'd need $500 to mass-produce some cassette tapes of our stuff. After we emptied our pockets, we barely had $80. The show was in ten days. We had to get that money, but how?

200

I was at work telling my boss about it and God opened his heart to the idea. The next thing I know, he was handing me the $500 and said, "Pay it back as soon as you can." I was stunned and thought he might be playing a joke on me, but he was a straight up serious guy.

"You can count on it!" I promised him.

I rushed the money to Discmakers and another miracle happened. The tapes arrived on the day of the first show. We performed both nights and were huge hits. We autographed tapes for hours, with people standing in line to get a piece of us. The Monday afterwards, I came to work and my boss said, "How was your event?"

I pulled out his $500, handed it to him, and said, "I can't thank you enough. Really, it was all God! He showed up in a big way!"

Amazed that I had paid it back so fast, he said, "Amen, brother!" and slapped me on the back. I could tell God was truly working in my life—we made over $2,000 from the event.

I met with Anthony and Mickell to give them their share and I don't know if we ever officially discussed it but from that point on, I jumped into action and started managing us as a group.

Soon I was hustling hard, making deals, setting up weekly gigs, and getting our music on the radio. I got DJ's to interview us and found bands to let us open for them. In fact, between working forty plus at Super Printers and making Christian rap music, I was gone just about every minute of every day. I rarely saw Neicy or my two children, but I was putting the pedal down and we were starting to make a few bucks at this. I could see that in the sea of music, my future was opening up like the Red Sea. All I had to do was follow God's lead.

This went on for over a year when a group from L.A. called the *S.S. Mob* came through town. By this time we had Portland sewed up and with God's help, I got us a gig opening for them. *S.S. Mob* was well known in the Christian community—they had a big record deal and performed all over the country. That night at the show, we killed it, and when the show was over, the band talked to us about moving to L.A., opening up for them at multiple venues (since they were playing in southern California a lot), and then going on the road. We said we'd talk about it and get back with them.

That night, we went back to my place pretty hyped about the possibility. Niecy was excited too, although she wasn't too keen on moving away from her family. Anthony and Mickell needed to talk to their loved ones about it, so we adjourned for the night. Before I was ready for bed, a late call came in from a buddy in Seattle.

"Hey Rose, you need to get home. Something's wrong with your Mom. I think I seen her being served on Union. I'm pretty sure it was her."

"What?! No way. She's clean and sober." Then I thought about how she hadn't returned my calls for over week. I'd been so busy landing this show that I'd forgotten Mom. I told him I'd check into it then hung up the phone. I dialed Mom's number and the answering machine picked up. *Again.* This was the fourth message I'd left. I sat down and thought for a minute. I knew what I had to do.

Still pumped from the show and the offer, I grabbed a small bag and stuffed some things in it. Then I went looking for my car keys. Neicy saw me. "What are you doing? It's after midnight."

"Baby, I got to run up to Seattle. Something's wrong. I need to check in with Mom. Besides, if nothing's wrong I need to tell her we're moving to L.A."
"But the boys haven't agreed yet."
"Don't worry they will," I said opening the front door.
"What about work?"
"I'll call them from Seattle and tell them what came up. He won't have a problem. I never take sick days or vacation time and I'm always there. This is family. He'll understand." With that, I closed the door and hit the road.

Two hours later—at 3:00 a.m.—I pulled up to my parent's apartment and saw a light on. I hoped someone was there. I knocked on the door, but no one answered. I still had a key so I let myself in. Immediately I saw drug paraphernalia everywhere along with half empty liquor bottles.

"Mom? Pops? Anyone here?"

The bathroom door was closed and the light was on. I heard some shuffling around. When she mumbled something, I knew it was Mom. I decided to wait for her to come out. The place was a disaster. Jamaine wasn't there. That told me all I needed to know. On the counter sat a blinking recorder. There were twenty-eight messages, so I began playing them. One by one there were people trying to get a hold of either Mom or Pops. A few were for Shelly. Mom staggered out of the bathroom as the messages were finishing. She looked like a zombie.

I grabbed her shoulders. "Mom, what's happened?"

She paused, staring at me hard. "Rose? Is that you, son?"

"Mom, it's me." I hugged her and she started crying. "Oh it's terrible," she wailed. "Terrible. They're all gone."

"Who's gone?"

"Them, all of them."

I lifted her chin. "Where's Desiree?"

"Gone."

"Where's Shelly?"

"Gone."

"Where's Pops?"

"Gone."

I looked around the apartment again trying to understand all this. Then I shook her. "Mom, did Shelly get her own place?"

"Oh no." She was doped up.

"And Pops? Is he runnin' the streets again?"

"No, he's with them."

"Who's them?"

"Shelly and Desiree."

"What?! That can't be. Why would he be with them?"

Mom licked her lips and her face grew dark and evil. "Because they been fucking each other right here under my nose!"

I let go and stepped back, almost falling down. Mom took a seat at the kitchen table and fumbled for a lighter.

"That can't be. No way! Mom are you sure?!"

"Oh yeah," she said her head unsteady. "Yeah, son, it's true."

"How do you know? How can you be sure?"

" 'Cus I caught them doin' it. He was on top of her and I recognized his thing, that's for sure."

I sat down next to her and tried to steady myself. Pops had run off with my old girl, my baby's momma. That's why he'd stared at his cards and didn't talk to me. Shelly had already been dropping her panties for him back then. I shook my head. "I knew she was low, but I didn't think she was that low."

"Oh yeah, honey. She took him 'cause she could. I took her in and that snake bit me."

My head was spinning. After extending a helping hand to this girl in her time of need, the seductive serpent struck again. This time her venom destroyed an entire family. Now Mom was staying drunk and high to numb the pain, and Jamaine was with Lavon again. My stomach burned, knowing my daughter was seeing all this too. I could do nothing about it. Nothing! I watched as she lit a joint. Then she put it to her lips and took a long pull. Her eyes rolled back as the feeling hit her. That's what she had been counting on. When she handed the joint to me, I took it and studied the raggedy tip at the end of my fingers. I thought of the feeling it would give me. All the pain it would numb. It had been so long since I had touched weed that I knew this first hit would really work well. I was now a man of God. I needed to lean on Him for help, not drugs. I had given all this up. Yet the joint lay right there, begging to be smoked. I swallowed hard and moved it closer to my lips. All I had to do was inhale and I could join Mom. Still, I hesitated. My new life told me no, but I had come from such a long line of misery, a heavy freight train of sin, a permanent pattern of self-destruction, all of which conspired to continually knock me down again and again. Sure, I'd gotten up each time and continued to fight for a better life, one devoted to God, but now I faced my toughest test so far. I knew the dark side was still very powerful in me, pushing me to lose myself in the weed, to let it takeover and run things. I knew that despite everything I'd recently accomplished, I was about to throw it all way and go back to the hood, the gansta life. That's the life decision I faced. Mom just faced it and made her choice. Now I had to make that choice and decide which way I was going to go. I shook my head fighting the urge to inhale then brought the joint up to my face, studied every detail in it, and made a decision.

## *Chapter Eleven*

There are three ways you hit the mat and become an underdog. The first is the most common: you make bad decisions that lead to bad results. Think drinking and driving. The second is due to circumstances over which you have no control. This happens to a great football player from a small school that doesn't get a college scholarship because no one knows he exists. Or a kid who is born in the ghetto whose parents have no money for college. Neither one of these guys did anything wrong yet they're still an underdog. The third is when the circumstances are stacked against you *and* you make bad decisions. This last one fit me perfectly. Sure, I'd been dealt a crappy hand but I'd been making a lot of bad decisions too. Really, I'd been an underdog from the day I was born and even though I showed signs of succeeding, I kept making bad decisions, which took me, right back to the bottom. Thankfully, God loves a good underdog. He'll even make them underdogs if He has to. Look no further than Gideon, Rahab, and David.

Gideon was a poor man threshing wheat in the field when God told him to go out and defeat a large army. He was scared and requested more and more signs from God to ensure he'd heard His command correctly. Each time God confirmed His instructions. When over thirty thousand men showed up to fight for Gideon, the Lord told him he had too many and needed to send home all those who were too afraid to fight. Over twenty-two thousand men left. Now down to ten thousand, Gideon prepared for battle yet the Lord told him he still had too many. When he had whittled the large group down to just three hundred, God said that that was plenty and it was. They destroyed a massive, entrenched enemy (with God's help of course).

Then there was the prostitute, Rahab, who hid the spies sent by Joshua. The spies were scouting out the city so Joshua could come and destroy it. Hiding these spies, Rahab could have easily been killed but she had one thing going for her: she recognized the one true God. When she helped them escape, she begged them to remember her when they attacked and destroyed the city. They did and spared her. Her reward was to be an ancestor to Jesus, a direct member of His bloodline.

The last example is a small shepherd boy. When no soldier in Saul's army would take up the gigantic Goliath's challenge to fight, this pint-sized kid named David stepped up and volunteered. King Saul tried to turn him away but he refused to leave. He was going to fight the giant. Then they tried to strap protection on him and give him weapons but again he refused. Why? Because he knew, being an underdog was no big deal as long as he had God. Walking towards him, Goliath laughed at the little unarmed boy approaching. Goliath had absolutely no fear for not only was he three times bigger than this kid but also metal covered almost every square inch of him. Then a small river stone whizzed through the air and sunk deeply into his unprotected forehead, sending him to the ground, flat on his face. With no other weapons, David moved in close, drew the unconscious Goliath's own sword, and stabbed him to death. Then, to make sure his victory was complete, he cut off his head and held it up. That's a true underdog—just what God loves.

Then there was me. I kept facing test after test and failing—miserably. At some point, surely God was going to give up on me. Or would I finally start doing the right thing and begin to accept the victories God was giving me?

I opened my eyes and saw the ugly, white stipple on the ceiling. At first, I wasn't sure where I was. I pulled the covers up to my chest and felt my head pounding. For a brief moment, I thought perhaps we were playing a gig somewhere and had shacked up with some friends. It took a few moments, but eventually the memories came trickling in through my screaming headache. I was on the couch in Mom's living room. I rubbed my temples. The smoke in the apartment was likely the culprit of my misery, although the long drive and lack of sleep didn't help. I thought back to last night—or actually early this morning. Then the pain of what had happened came alive again as I remembered everything.

Just a few hours earlier, I was holding that joint up to my mouth and about to go back to my old life, a life based on the flesh. The anger inside me had burned hotly. Not only was I deeply hurt and confused, I felt the highest level of betrayal possible—my own father. This was a new low for Shelly too. It was tough to keep my hands wrapped around God and not let go. Holding that joint, I had felt my hands slipping off Him. I had even glanced down and saw the dark pit I was about to fall into. However, like David, I felt the spirit of God come over me, giving me the strength to put that joint down and refuse to give in to my flesh. Finally, I was not going to be defeated. This underdog was going to slay his Goliath.

With a clear head, I had pushed the joint away and just sat there talking to Mom about God, hoping and praying some of it would take root. I could see this final act of Pop's had broken whatever fragile thread of hope she'd still had inside her. All the criminal acts, the drug smuggling, and the abandonment she'd suffered from him...like Shelly, he lived to use and abuse those around him. In short, he lived for the flesh. Nothing else. If any one of us got too close or tried to hang onto him (or Shelly), we were taken under to drown in our own misplaced faith. Without God to protect us, we were dead to our sins. It was through all this haze that I finally understood that I couldn't save Mom. It didn't matter how hard I tried. She still rejected the only true savior, Jesus. Pops' final act had completely broken her spirit, sending her to the only two saviors she knew: alcohol and drugs. It was just a continuing tragedy for yet another anonymous person in the hood, another underdog who would always stay on the mat.

I left Seattle that afternoon and hit Portland around six. I was heading home when a 1980 Malibu Classic pulled up next to me at a stop light. I snapped my head over and stared hard at the driver. He could see me looking at him and tried to ignore me. When the light turned green, I followed him. Sure enough, it was my old car; the one that was supposed to take us to the abortion clinic, the one that wouldn't start. The Malibu traveled about three miles with me right on its tail when it suddenly swerved to the right and pulled into a neighborhood where it obviously didn't belong. Halfway down the block, the driver slammed on the brakes and jumped out of the car waving his arms at me and yelling. "What's your problem, man?! Huh?!" I got out and slowly approached him. "Where did you get this car?"

He was still agitated. "I saw it was abandoned so I went to the DMV and got an abandoned vehicle title. Then I had it towed to a shop and fixed. Why?"
I held my hands up. "Okay bro, but this used to be my car. I left it there because it wouldn't run."
"Well, you got a problem with me now?! Huh? I got the title. It's mine."

I tried to calm him down. "No problem, it's all yours buddy. Go ahead and keep rolling. I don't want any trouble. I just wanted to know if this really was my old car. This car actually saved a life, that's all. It sure did." I got back in my car and drove away, leaving him standing behind my car...or actually *his* car now. The incident just showed me how funny it was that God allowed me to see it one more time, to remind me of how *He* had saved my daughter's life, not the car. When I got home, I didn't tell Neicy about it. This was something I wanted to keep to myself.

***

To my surprise just two weeks later, I received a call from mom. She said that she had been thinking of all that we spoke about and she was ready to make that change. She wanted to give her life to Jesus, get off the mat, and be victorious. She had just got my baby brother Jamaine back from Lavon and asked me to come and pick her up to get them away from all the madness that surrounded them. I was so excited that without hesitation I rushed back to Seattle to pick them up and bring them back with me where they lived for the next couple of months until mom got on her feet. This was the change that she needed. She turned from the drugs, alcohol, and she never looked back.

A few months later, Neicy, Mickell, and I hit the road for L.A. We left our kids with Margaret and found a place to share in Moreno Valley. At first, Anthony didn't come with us but later he joined us. By now, I was twenty-one and Neicy was nineteen. Being so young, we found L.A. to be one overwhelming place, something we'd have to get used to for us to live there.

The band we'd come down for quickly started experiencing problems and fell apart. This left us on our own. Before we got too far along in our music career, we talked about the name *S.4.G* and knew if we were ever going to change it, now would be the time. We agreed to change it to *Christsyde*.

We began touring and playing venues everywhere. It was both fun and grueling. By now, we had the two kids with us, so often Neicy stayed at home while I performed. As incredibly talented as he was, Anthony was dealing with some issues and we all decided that it would be best if he didn't move forward with the group. Since many gigs were on the weekend, one thing I did to make sure the money kept flowing was to get a job. Pro Printing put me to work as their bindery guy. When they saw what I could do, they transitioned me over to operating a printing press, which became my job for several years after that. Having a job freed up Neicy to stay home and raise the kids. That was very important to me.

VICTORIOUS UNDERDOG

One day I got a call from my brother Lavon to tell me Pops had had another kid—with Shelly. My baby's momma had a baby with my father, which was now my half-sister. So now, my oldest daughter and I share a sister. Wow! Talk about messed up. Mom still had a hard time, but seemed to be slowing down on the liquor and weed. It was finally dawning on her that Pops was gone for good.

Soon after, Neicy got pregnant and gave birth to our third child. We named her Janell. Now I had four children. Desiree was my oldest. Sadly, my relationship with her was nonexistent. For six long years, I had tried to see her and talk to her. Each time I got a hold of Shelly she'd say Desiree doesn't want to talk to me and hung up the phone. For all that, time Desiree believed I'd rejected her. Since Shelly was living with Pops, it was a bad situation for me and for Desiree too. I just didn't know how to fix it.

As far as our music careers, we had gigs every weekend all over Southern California and sometimes had to fly out to other states. Many of the places we played were churches, before many young people. We quickly discovered that in each location, the young people couldn't get enough of Christian rap. That excited me because we were right there with all the popular names in Christian music.

To spread our name even further, I began seeking out gigs in cities we hadn't been before. And I found an edge. In every city we hit, the day we arrived, Mickell and I would set up on a street corner in the ghetto and start rapping. Sometimes we'd hit the projects and perform in the courtyard. In no time a crowd would form, giving us the chance to spread God's message and urge them to attend the show. This always brought more people to the venue to hear us. When the promoter who signed us up to play there heard the kids screaming for us, it made it look like we were well known and sometimes we were.

Each year I sent out tons of demo tapes and, as a result, we'd landed gigs everywhere and made appearances on TBN and BET. By now, we'd met all the main players in the Christian rap industry and they all knew us. Almost all the groups loved sharing the stage with us.

One day we got a call from *Rescue Records* out of San Diego, which one of the fathers of a member of P.O.D ran. P.O.D. was also signed to the label. They asked us if we would be interested in being label mates with P.O.D. There were also a few other big names from that time on the label such as Tonex and Unity Klan. We said yes and instantly, *Christsyde* had a record deal.

At first, when people hear you've signed a record deal, it sounds like you hit the big time. And it can be, but for us, it wasn't. The folks on the other side of our deal were a lot smarter than we were. When we signed, I thought they'd spend lots of money to market us, get us bigger gigs, and get us studio time for better albums. That's why we ignorantly agreed to give them 90% of the sales profits. Instead, our sales slumped because they weren't doing anything. Unless we found a gig to play, we didn't get one. For this, we gave them 90%. They were smart and saw how many gigs we had pulled in for ourselves so they decided to take a free cut. We fell for it because it sounded so great to tell people we had a record deal. Lesson learned.

We suffered through the contract. At the end of two years, we were outta there. When we took over again, things started to get back to the way they were before the deal. Soon after, we started our own label *Christsyde Records, C.S.R* and began looking for talent to sign. Quickly we snatched up a nice distribution deal through the same company that had distributed the label we'd just left. I called the owner directly and convinced him to spend the money to promote us. He agreed.

Later I created *C.S.R. Entertainment* for the movies we planned to get into. This was a big move and took a lot of time and energy. Unfortunately, I spent less and less time back home with Neicy. The reality was this was my dream, not hers. "I am tired of living your life. I want to live my own life." That was her constant refrain. I fought her for years but finally said, okay. Even though I was completely faithful to her the whole time we were married, it just wasn't enough to sustain us. By now, we both knew that if we'd met each other for the first time, we wouldn't be interested in each other at all. We had both completely changed and we were no longer close to a version of who we were when we first met. So at twenty-seven years old, I got divorced.

At the time, I thought because I was doing something positive with my talents that everything would always be perfect and never would I have predicted getting divorced. Looking back I know I wasn't a very good husband, especially since I was hardly ever home. That's a tough way to build a lasting relationship.

One thing I got out of the divorce was the opportunity to raise my kids because I had custody of them. Each morning, I'd drop my baby Janell off at preschool then go to work at the print shop. I was making decent money there and I feared leaving that job and counting solely on the music money. I was good friends with the owner so he'd let me pick up Janell from preschool in the afternoons and bring her back to work where she'd sit in the lobby and watch movies while I finished the day. Then I'd go home where my two other kids were already there and cook dinner. I discovered I was a natural in the kitchen and over the years developed to be quite the cook.

During all this, several folks blessed me by helping keep an eye on my children when I needed to go out of town. When I wasn't on the road, I spent a lot of time in my recording studio. Usually Janell came to the studio with me and watched me work. She was so cute sitting there moving to beat. That really made me smile no matter how bad my day was going.

By now, Shelly had moved to Indiana with Desiree. One weekend I had a gig there and called ahead to tell her I'd be there. I wanted to see Desiree. Shelly said Desiree didn't want to see me, but I told her I'd come and get her anyway. She reluctantly agreed to bring her to the venue. Sure enough, Shelly showed up with my daughter. I couldn't believe it. I talked privately with Desiree, who was now twelve, and explained how I hadn't heard from her. Of course, she'd had no idea I'd even called. She was stunned I'd mailed a plane ticket for her to come and see me. She never got that either.

Shelly had continued with her wickedness, but it wasn't as if she had changed from the very first time she'd dropped her panties for me. It was my fault because from the beginning—my own lust blinded me. She'd never changed and I shouldn't have ever expected her to. The enemy was too embedded in her. Desiree and I visited the rest of the time and she saw me perform. I hugged her goodbye and laid some cash in her hands. A year later, I received a call from Shelly's mother telling me Desiree was in with the wrong crowd. "You need to get your daughter!" she said.

My immediate response was, "Send her my way." The truth was, I'd been praying to God for this very thing. It was the only way to reconcile with her. When she landed in L.A., I hugged her so hard I didn't want to let go. With my three kids from Neicy and my oldest from Shelly all living with me, I had the original full house. God was great!

## *Chapter Twelve*

In 2002, I could really see God's work in my life. He'd blessed me with a somewhat successful music career. The entertainment company that I started along with our road manager Maggie Gardner, who is also my spiritual mother, was just getting started. I was making good money but not enough yet to leave my printing job. I began signing up other acts. We actually marketed them! From my experience with door-to-door sales, I put together street teams to sell a lot of product. With more and more money coming in, we decided to invest it back into the business rather than spend it on flashy cars or other junk we didn't need.

One of the first things we decided to invest in was our own recording studio. As it was, we had to pay stiff fees to rent studios for time and I was tired of it. By owning our own studio and equipment, we not only saved money, we made it! This way my groups had all the studio time they needed and when we weren't using it, we rented it out to other groups.

To better shore up my financial end on the personal side, I looked at my current housing situation. I was paying a high rent to have just an ok apartment for my children and me. One day, Sean, my close friend and DJ, approached me about a problem he was having. He was going through a divorce and experiencing money problems. It turned out that he owned a large trailer where he and his two children lived. It wasn't the nicest place but it was a home. I suggested that I move in with my family and pay him rent. This would help him with his expenses and we could be roommates— two single men raising our own kids. We could help each other out, keep an eye on the kids, and divide the bills and chores. I also knew that the more money I saved, the more I could put back into my business. Sean agreed. As an added bonus, the trailer was in the middle of nowhere. This meant our children weren't tempted to get into trouble. For the kids and me, it turned out to be a great move.

This arrangement went on for a year while I spent all my time working at the print shop and hustling gigs and entertainment deals. Eventually, I had not only saved up enough money but I was making good money too. I got a tip on a nice little house that was for rent back in Moreno Valley so I moved my family back there. Meanwhile, I was regularly calling on all the TV shows to see if I could get one of my acts or myself on. Then one day I picked up the phone and it was a lady named Marci Kenan. She told me that she was producing a documentary film called Higher Ground that would be highlighting the faces of contemporary Gospel music. She was familiar with the projects that I had been a part of with Christsyde and wanted us to be a part of the project. Well I agreed instantly but since I was making the transition from performer to label executive I put an option other than Christsyde on the table. C. L. Ryderz (Christ Life Ryderz) was a fresh new group that I believed would change the game. The documentary presented Christsyde and C. L. Ryderz did all the promo for the film. We set out on a complete campaign of radio and television publicity spots. In the midst of the campaign trail was *Soul Train*. They wanted *C. L. Ryderz* to be on the show. They told me this would be the first time they had ever had a Christian rap group perform. With God's help, we would break new ground.

My group and I showed up and there was a star on the door saying 'C. L. Ryderz.' The door next to ours said *En Vogue*, a popular all-girl R&B group. Man, it felt like we'd made it. When *Soul Train's* founder and executive producer Don Cornelius introduced himself to us, we didn't think life could get any better. The show went off perfectly and C. L. Ryderz got a boost that we had not yet seen. As soon as it aired, my phone exploded with more deals. We landed big concerts and many lucrative deals. I took advantage of this burst of good fortune and signed up even more acts, sending them out on tour to spread God's message.

Right in the midst of a road trip, I received a call from Auntie Pam telling me that my grandma Georgia had passed away. Grandma died on the floor in her apartment back in Stockton. This devastated me so bad that I couldn't even speak. This woman believed in me more than anyone else in the world did and I lost a piece of my soul that day. I broke away from the tour and headed back to my hometown for a few days to lay grandma to rest. Losing someone close to you is never easy and I had been through so much in my past on my own but now I knew the power of Jesus and that I didn't have to bear this pain alone. I prayed and trusted God to help me keep my head up through this time and He did exactly that. I was able to catch up with my crew and it was back to business as we finished the tour.

My business partner Maggie controlled the money and most of it went into travel expenses, product, equipment, and keeping the wheels turning on the label. I still continued working at the printing company and made plenty of extra cash hustling CD's on the streets with the street team. I was simply too cautious to give up that guaranteed income. Besides, management was easy on me—they loved having me as an employee. This got me thinking: what more can I do for God? He's been so good to me. There has to be more I can do.

Sure enough, He pointed out an opportunity. Moreno Valley, California was in desperate need of something to reach all those young people they had roaming around, young people easily led astray. With the money I was making off the music business, I decided to set up my own youth church—the New G Hip-Hop Church. The big idea was to have the kind of worship service that would attract young people. This meant having Christian rappers perform. The good news was that I knew just about everyone in this industry. It really felt like this was something God was pushing me to do.

I located a church that would allow us to sublease from them just to get the ball rolling. We threw a huge grand opening party once we got everything set up and Kurtis Blow, the Legendary Rap Icon turned Minister, showed up as my invited guest speaker. Kurtis Blow was the first commercial rapper ever to land a major record deal. With his presence—and *His* presence—It turned out to be an amazing night. New Generation Hip Hop Church was born and great things would follow. This was something fresh, something that many had never seen before. Young people were flocking to the services and many changed through the power of God.

The L. A. Times did a cover story of this crazy thing that was happening in Moreno Valley. I even appeared on *The Evening News* with Katie Couric. Compared to all the terrible things I'd been involved in earlier, my life surely glorified God now.

I now spent all of my time with the church, the music business, and raising my family. Each day I tried to bring as many new lost souls to Christ as I possibly could. I was the fisherman and He provided the boat and the net. All I had to do was cast it out there and let God do His work. Man, it was an amazing thing to see! After a short time, I knew everyone in the community. The parents loved what I was doing with their kids and spread the news all over the country, which opened up even more gigs. One such gig was a youth encounter event in Michigan. A thousand kids showed up to hear us perform five times in two days. Like every event, I told them how I got away from the devil and that they could too. I could see this affect them. Christ was working overtime. When it was over, they gave us a great sendoff to our next concert where we repeated it all over again.

During breaks from performing, I'd check the computer and see emails from all around the world including the U.K., Germany, and even Russia. These people loved what we were doing. Each time I returned to Cali, there were bunches of letters to open. One time I opened a letter from a thirteen-year-old girl. She told me she'd come to that huge youth event in Michigan and planned on committing suicide in the hotel bathtub. Her idea was to have her youth leader and all of her peers find her dead body. She wanted them to understand how much she had hated her life. When she saw us and heard our message, it broke her down completely and she realized that her life was not that bad. During one of our performances there, she decided to live and share her story too. Letters like that kept me hustling and working hard for God.

Life was rolling smooth and everything I touched seemed to turn to gold. Then one day as I was on my knees in prayer, the words of Mark 11:26 began to ring continuously in my mind. "But if you do not forgive, neither will your Father who is in heaven forgive your transgressions." At that moment, God was giving me the grace, capacity, genuine love, and ability to forgive everyone who had wronged me in any way. As I ran down the list of people that I thought I needed to forgive, it seemed as though I could feel myself getting lighter from releasing the weight of whatever grudges I may have been holding. Then it hit me. I thought of Shelly and my Pops. I had to pause. My Pops had taken my ex-girl, had sex and produced a child with her, destroyed my Mom, treated me like a piece of crap, and did just about every evil thing known to man. Shelly was guilty of all the same. Then I thought of all that I had done and all that God had already forgiven me for and now has allowed me to have such a blessed life. I knew that this was required of me now. I released them both from the grudge and hard feelings that I had been harboring for all these years. The power of God overwhelmed me with true forgiveness and love and I literally felt the weight lift off me. I immediately reached for my phone and called my dad's number. I knew that he and Shelly were a thing of the past now and they had gone their separate ways.

"Hey Pops how are you?"
"I'm good It's been a long time man, how are you?" I could tell he was shocked to hear from me.
"I'm blessed, the reason that I'm calling is because I want you to know that whatever happened between us in the past, all that you've done and all that we've been through doesn't matter to me anymore. I forgive you, I don't hold anything against you now, and I never will. And I'm asking you to forgive me for any hurtful things that I may have said or done over the years."
There was a few seconds of silence.
"Pops you still there?"
"Yea I'm here"
I knew my Pops was no good with the mushy sensitive stuff so to ease his discomfort I rushed off the phone.
"Yo are we good now? I gotta run but I just wanted to tell you that ok?"
"Yea son we're good."
Later I tracked down Shelly's number and had a similar talk with her.

## *Chapter Thirteen*

The world felt a lot lighter now and I started traveling up to Stockton more often to spend time with my Pops. We caught up with our lives and mostly talked about my career. He had seen me on TV and told everyone in the hood that that was his son. He wanted to know what performing before huge audiences was like and for once, was truly interested in me. It was yet another gift from God.

No matter where I was performing, I always tried to make sure I was home to perform and preach at New G. If I couldn't make it, I had other great preachers who would fill in and give hard-hitting messages. With the different performing artists that I knew, I could rotate them through the church to keep things fresh. Everything was working perfectly.

Things continued like this for a couple of years, and then I began seeing a different world. Sales of our music had fallen. Less and less people were showing up to concerts—any concert—and organizers began cutting back. It's almost as if things evaporated overnight. Now we had fewer gigs, and the ones we had were half-full. Instead of selling and autographing two hundred CD's after a concert, we now sold maybe ten— and that was on a good night. I started hearing about massive layoffs and people losing their homes. We weren't even able to bring in good money from street CD sales, which are what I, relied heavy on to keep things flowing.

Eventually we had to shut the doors and I headed to Texas to regroup and start over—again.

By this time, Desiree was almost twenty-one and had already moved into her own place. My son Rico had been getting into trouble hanging with the wrong crowds. He decided he needed to get out of California so he took off to live with his grandma Margaret back in Portland. Neicy had settled down in Atlanta and agreed to take our two youngest daughters Arkita and Janell. Now I was the only one I had to look out for, so I made up my mind and took the haul with my God-parents, Maggie and Clarence on their retirement plan and landed in Mansfield, Texas in September of 2010. Fed up with the uncertainty of the music business, I decided to go after a stable career. I always knew that if I had to start over with a new career that I'd want to cook professionally because I was good at it. I immediately registered for the Associates Degree Program at Le Cordon Bleu Culinary College and jumped head first into the next chapter of my life.

To save money, my plan was to stay with Maggie and Clarence for a few months. I picked up a job at a Neiman-Marcus warehouse in Irving packing orders. It wasn't what I was shooting for, but it kept me going while I was in school and planning my next steps. In December that year, just before Christmas I got word my grandmother Daisy (my father's mother) had passed away. Another devastating blow, we were losing all of our family matriarchs. Once again, I headed back to Stockton to lay my other grandma to rest.

My Pops was one of the toughest men that I knew but he was no match for standing strong in the face of losing his mother. During the funeral, he collapsed to the floor. Figuring he was having trouble dealing with the death of his mother my brothers and I lifted him up and helped him walk outside to get some air. He was holding his chest and having difficulty breathing. An ambulance took him to the hospital and we stayed back to finish the service for grandma. After burying grandma, I went to the hospital to see Pops lying in the hospital bed. He only looked tired, not at all sick. One of my cousins told me that Pops had fluid or mucus around his lungs like pneumonia or something like that. I left to let him rest and when I returned the next day he was awake and back to his normal, playful self. He told me that in a couple of days they were going to perform a procedure where they would stick tubes down his throat and suck out the mucus. He spoke of it as a simple procedure, then we talked about him coming to visit me in Texas when this was all over. I sat there with him for a few hours and we laughed, joked, and talked about everything. We spent the best quality time together ever. When it was time for me to leave, we said our goodbyes and I was on my way. I had a plane to catch back to Dallas soon but I wanted to stop by my Auntie Clara's (Pops' older sister) before I left. When I went into her house, I saw her sitting there with this blank look on her face.

"Are you okay, Auntie?"

No words came out as she shook her head slowly back and forth in saying "NO" motion.

I realized that her mother was just put to rest and the day has been quite eventful with what Pops is dealing with now so I didn't want to push her. However, I could tell that there was something else on her mind.

"Auntie, what's going on?"

Then she came out with it.

"The Doctors say there's nothing else that can be done. His organs are slowly shutting down and it's just a matter of time now. We have to start planning for his service."

"What! No, No, No way!" I said

"I was just with him and he's perfectly fine, we we're laughing, joking, and he was his normal self. There's no way!"

Auntie Clara explained to me that my Pops had lung cancer and it was in the final stages.

I didn't believe her. I called Pops to hear his voice and confirm with him that I was right. I couldn't get the words together to ask him if he had cancer so instead I asked him if he was certain he wanted to come see me in Texas when this was all over.

He said, "Absolutely, just let me get through this procedure and we'll pick right up"

"Ok love you, Pops, talk to you later."

"Love you too, Son."

I believed him. He appeared too strong and healthy to be on his deathbed so I hopped on the plane and went back to Dallas. I spoke to him on the phone the day before he went in to surgery. When he came out, he couldn't speak well enough to talk on the phone because the tubes had scratched his throat somehow so we never spoke after that. I always thought of him as being invincible and I knew for sure that he would pull through this. Two weeks later, just three weeks after my grandmother died, I got the call that Pops had passed away. A whirlwind of emotions hit me. I was angry because he carried this disease and never told any of us. He robbed us of any opportunity to help him. I felt the sting of losing someone close again just weeks after losing grandma. I was sorrowful that I spent so many years angry and not speaking to him. Then I was so grateful to God that we were able to reconcile and be close at the end.

Again, I went back to Stockton for yet another funeral. When I returned to Dallas, I continued with school and soon landed a job as a doorman at a place called Deloitte University. By the time I earned my degree I had already been promoted twice and was making more money than they would pay me to work in the kitchen and I was quickly on my way to management and that's where I ended up for another two years. When I moved on from that, I went into social work and became a Case Manager for troubled youth in Dallas.

As for my old homies, some of them were incarcerated, some died, and some simply disappeared. As for me, I was one who'd made it out of that bucket of crabs and found a different life. The difference maker for me is my corner man, someone there by my side giving me advice, courage, and perseverance. Someone to step in the ring with me and strap on my gloves of righteousness and faithfulness. That someone has made all the difference. In fact, He suffered and died for me so that I could have eternal life.

Now it's time for my message to you. It's my prayer that if you haven't done so already, you would accept Christ as your personal savior by sincerely saying these words:

"Lord Jesus, please forgive me of my sins as I now place my faith in you as God's Son, the one who died on the cross for me, so that I may have eternal life. I fully accept you, Jesus Christ, as my Lord and Savior. Please help me live for you. Amen."

Made in the USA
Charleston, SC
03 December 2016